WHAT HAPPENS AT MASS

REVISED EDITION

JEREMY DRISCOLL, OSB

GRACEWING

First published in 2005
jointly by

Gracewing Publishing
2 Southern Avenue
Leominster
Herefordshire HR6 0QF
England

Liturgy Training Publications
Archdiocese of Chicago
1800 North Hermitage Avenue
Chicago, Il 60622-1101
USA

Nihil Obstat
Reverend Brian J. Fischer, STL
Censor Deputatus
September 20, 2004

Imprimatur
Most Reverend Raymond E. Goedert, MA, STL, JCL
Vicar General
Archdiocese of Chicago
September 24, 2004

The *Nihil Obstat* and *Imprimatur* are official declarations that a book is free of doctrinal and moral error. No implication is contained therein that those who have granted the *Nihil Obstat* and *Imprimatur* agree with the content, opinions, or statement expressed. Nor do they assume any legal responsibility associated with publication.

UK ISBN 978-0-85244-637-9

Cover art by Brother Claude Lane, OSB, of Mount Angel Abbey. The icon depicts "the disciple whom Jesus loved, who reclined close to him as they ate" (John 13:23).

Contents

Introduction   v

Chapter One   Laying the Groundwork,
                 Establishing the Context   1

Chapter Two   The Introductory Rites   17

Chapter Three The Liturgy of the Word   29

Chapter Four   The Preparation of the Gifts   59

Chapter Five   The Eucharistic Prayer   68

Chapter Six   Communion   106

Chapter Seven The Concluding Rites   128

A Summary   131

Introduction

The title for this book was given to me by a friend who has a talent for coming up with good titles for almost anything: books, articles, poems, paintings, but also movies, which he is always renaming with more successful titles. He knew of other things I had written about the Eucharist during a number of years, articles and books aimed at an academic audience for discussion. Now my friend was urging that I write a book directed toward a different group. He was persuading me to write a non-academic book for any Catholic interested simply in understanding the Mass better. He said, "We're losing track of what it is. It's not clear any more. We need someone just to tell us again." Then he gave me this title: *What Happens at Mass*. I liked this title. It is clear, and it defines the project. I want to speak in a simple and straightforward manner. I want to show what the Mass means and where its center is. And I want to stress this word *happens* in the title, for indeed that is the point. Something happens at Mass. God is acting! He acts to save us. It is a huge event. In fact, there is nothing bigger. God has concentrated the entirety of His saving love for the world into the ritual action and words of the Eucharistic liturgy. I want to speak of the Mass in these terms.

If I try to speak as simply as possible, I will still be speaking about something that cannot be named, or cannot easily be named, something we call mystery. So I will aim to speak without losing the sense of mystery, for there is no resolving it. But there is a deeper entry into it and a way of learning to move within its spaces. This is what I hope to offer here: deeper entry and a certain grace of movement within the forms.

It goes without saying that we do not understand the Mass as well as we should, but it would be a mistake to think that the Mass should be immediately understandable to all. How could it be? It is the summit of the Christian life. One does not begin at the summit; a summit is arrived at slowly and with effort. People—believers and unbelievers alike—cannot expect to come in off the street and demand to have something immediately meaningful to them. And who defines meaningful in any case? I will not get very far in understanding the Mass if I think I have the right to have it be meaningful to me in ways that I define. That would take away all possibility of receiving the Mass as a gift from another, from God. He defines it. It is His initiative, His action.

The Mass is a ritual, and this means that it requires initiation, repetition, a sense of performance. There is a gradual deepening of its sense. A right attitude toward it is needed and must be learned. Ritual could perhaps best be described as a kind of serious play. For example, I am willing to go along with the ritual—all the set movements and words repeated in a certain way—because I trust that when I "play this way" something great and unexpected can break through. The ritual is a form, and the form delivers a content—not an intellectual content to be grasped with the mind, but an actual event, nothing less than the very event of our salvation. If I refuse to join in the "game"; that is, if I refuse the ritual and its rules and forms, then I am left only as I came. It's just me; it's only us; what can happen is only the sum of the parts. But the ritual takes us out of ourselves and beyond ourselves. It lets God act and gives us a way of acting in response. We don't have to invent the response, coming up with it on the spot. How pitiable that would be! Instead, the ritual gives us a response adequate to the mystery of what the ritual has also delivered; namely, God's own saving action. In this book, therefore, I will be examining the ritual. I will look at what we say and do during the Mass, and I will try to say something about all that happens when we say and do that. Paradoxically, to go more deeply into the meaning of the Mass, we must remain also always on the surface, never leaving behind its actual forms. For the very forms themselves—the bread, the wine, the movements of the priest and people—become completely imbued with significance, with divine life itself.

The Mass is about love. It is not an idea about love but the supreme encounter with love. A Christian is defined entirely by this encounter. And so, I am not in the world as in Descartes' notion: I think, therefore I am, or as a variation on this theme, something to the effect of: I love, therefore I am. Rather, because of what happens at Mass, I know what it is that makes me to be: I am loved, therefore I am. For this I give thanks together with all others who know their existence to be defined in this way.

To say that the Mass is about love is to say that it is an encounter. It is an encounter with God, but not God as vaguely conceived. It is an encounter with God through Jesus. We encounter Jesus, and through him we encounter the one whom he calls God and Father. We do not encounter Jesus as vaguely conceived. Our encounter with him is nothing less than an encounter with one whom we must also call Lord and God. These are not arbitrary designations of Jesus, ideas floated during the course of a ceremony. The Jesus who was crucified under Pontius Pilate and whose Death is remembered during the course of the Mass is encountered there as risen from the dead and so known as Lord and God. This precisely defined encounter with God gives me freedom. It defines me. It offers me a new self in which I am defined through this new relationship. It is the very opposite of original sin, for original sin is wanting to be myself by myself alone and not through relationship with God.

Every true relationship needs to be experienced. Mass is the foundational experience of our relationship with God through Jesus, experienced and celebrated in all its fullness. This experience renders possible all other relationships. That is, it makes it possible for us to love others as we have been loved by God.

* * *

After an introductory chapter to establish the overall context, the book's arrangement simply follows the order of Mass, the way in which the ritual in each of its parts unfolds. The Mass begins with Introductory Rites and ends with Concluding Rites. Between these lie the two major parts, referred to as the Liturgy of the Word and the Liturgy of the Eucharist. These major parts of the liturgy form the major parts of the book.

Chapter One

Laying the Groundwork, Establishing the Context

The method of this book, as I have said, will be to concentrate on the ritual shape of the Mass. But the first dimension of such a task must be to establish the context of the ritual. There are four different things that will prepare us for a better discussion of the rite itself. First, we will want to see how the Church uses the words *mystery* and *sacrament* in reference to the liturgy and in reference to theology in general. Second, there is the significance of the people assembling for Mass. Third, we will discuss the overarching shape or movement of the entire rite, which—a surprise perhaps—will require our speaking of the mystery of the Holy Trinity. Fourth, something should be said about imagining an ideal celebration as necessary for the way we want to conduct our reflection so that we don't get tangled up in questions of a practical nature.

MYSTERY AND SACRAMENT

One of the most beautiful and exciting and multilayered terms that Christians use to celebrate and think about their faith is the word mystery. So it is important to understand how the term has been used and is still used inside the faith. We cannot let this understanding be determined and limited by what the term may mean in contemporary language and usage. There it tends to mean something difficult, if not impossible, to understand. Or it can refer to a genre of story with parts that do not fit together easily and which must somehow be resolved.

It is only in a sense vaguely related to these meanings that Christians use the word mystery, and it is better to try to understand it from the history of its application.

From the time of the apostles, the Christian community celebrated the rites of Baptism and Eucharist in obedience to the Lord's commands (Matthew 28:19; Luke 22:19). From as early as the second century, these rites were referred to as mysteries. But why? A deep intuition and insight is carried in the application of this word to those ritual practices. The roots of the intuition lie in the theology of Saint Paul, who used the word *mystery* as a key concept in his whole understanding of what had happened in Christ. For Saint Paul the central mystery is the Cross of Christ. But why does he call the Cross a mystery? He does so to express that something was hidden in the Cross which we cannot understand without its being revealed. As he explains in the second chapter of the first letter to the Corinthians, when "the rulers of this age" crucified Christ, they did not understand who he was, for his true identity was hidden. But in fact the rulers of this age crucified "the Lord of Glory." This is because, as he said, "None of the rulers of this age knew the mystery. If they had known it, they would never have crucified the Lord of Glory" (1 Corinthians 7–8).

Yet for Saint Paul it is not only the Lord of Glory that is hidden in the cross of Christ. So much unfolds from the cross, which to all appearances is but the ignominious death of a criminal. But, as Saint Paul explains, "I know what I am talking about in speaking of the mystery of Christ, unknown in former ages but now revealed by the Spirit to the holy apostles and prophets. It is no less than this: in Christ Jesus the Gentiles are now co-heirs with the Jews, members of the same body and sharers of the promise through the preaching of the gospel" (Ephesians 3:4–6). In fact, the entire plan of God for the world is hidden in the cross. So it is that Paul can announce the Christian message as the gift of being given "the wisdom to understand fully the mystery, the plan he was pleased to decree in Christ" (Ephesians 1:9). What that plan is was not plain to any and all who looked at Christ, and so it is a mystery. But to those who understand the mystery, it was nothing less than "all things in heaven and on earth recapitulated in Christ" (Ephesians 1:10). Christ himself is called "the mystery of God" because "in him every treasure of wisdom and knowledge is hidden" (Colossians 2:2–3).

So, always something hidden but now something also revealed. Although Saint Paul does not put it quite the way I am about to put it, I think the following is a fair way of summarizing the huge world of thought that swirls around his use of the word *mystery*. This summary gets us some way toward understanding how the same word came to be used for Baptism and Eucharist. I would say that a mystery is a concrete something that when you bump into it, it puts you in contact with a divine reality. The Cross is a concrete something; in it is the Lord of Glory. The history of Israel is a concrete something; in it is the promise also for the Gentiles. Everything in heaven and on earth is a concrete something; it is all destined to be recapitulated in Christ. Applying the same logic to Baptism and Eucharist, we could say that being plunged into water and brought up again three times is a concrete something; in it is hidden a believer's dying and rising with Christ. The bread and wine of the Eucharist are concrete somethings; in them are hidden the very Body and Blood of Christ. All of these things then are called mysteries.

If we use a phrase like "the mystery of the Eucharist," this does not mean that which cannot be understood about the Eucharist. It means that the Eucharist is a concrete something in which a divine reality is hidden. If we use the word in the singular, "mystery of the Eucharist," it refers to the rite as a whole. But the Eucharist was and is also called "the mysteries," and here the reference is to the various dimensions working together. The gestures, the words, the bread and wine, the members of the assembly in their various roles—all of these are mysteries. In them is hidden the Lord of Glory. This is why at the very beginning of the Mass, the bishop or priest urges the assembly,

"Brethren (brothers and sisters), let us acknowledge our sins, / and so prepare ourselves to celebrate the sacred mysteries." Or in the very center of the intensity of the Eucharistic Prayer, he exclaims, "The mystery of faith," and all the people proclaim what is hidden in the consecrated bread and wine; namely, that by his Cross and Resurrection, he has set us free.

Hopefully this serves to help us recover a meaningful use of the word *mystery* for our celebration. I will use the word often in what follows, and we all need confidently to reawaken this particular Christian usage in our talk about these things, about these mysteries. It is worth adding here that it is with the same understanding that we use the word in reference to the mysteries of the rosary. There the mysteries are concrete events from the life of Christ, in all of which divine realities are hidden. We also use the word to refer to the central content of Christian faith: the mystery of the Holy Trinity. Again, this does not mean that which we cannot understand about the Trinity. It means that in the concrete life of Jesus is hidden and now revealed the one God: Father, Son, and Holy Spirit. The concrete life of Jesus, as this culminates in his Death, is called the Paschal Mystery, meaning that from his Death unfolds the Resurrection, the Ascension, the sending of the Spirit, the Church. In all of these usages—from Saint Paul, to the Eucharist, to the rosary, to the Paschal Mystery, to the Trinity—the word *mystery* preserves the tension between the concrete and the divine. Something is definitely present, but what is present exceeds and overflows the limits of the concrete, even if it is present only by means of it. This is mysterious in a way unique to Christian understanding. As I said above, there is no resolving the mystery. But there is a deeper entry into it and a way of learning to move within its spaces. It is that which I hope to offer here: deeper entry and a certain grace of movement within the mysteries.

In the history of theology the word *sacrament* is closely related to *mystery.* The origin of the English *mystery* is the Greek word *mysterion,* and there is a Latin word that directly translates it: *mysterium*. But our English word *sacrament* comes from the Latin *sacramentum*, and there is no Greek equivalent. We, with our roots in the Latin tradition, call some liturgical rites sacraments; and we have seen that we also call them mysteries. The Greeks have only one word for what we call sacraments; they always call them mysteries. But in the Latin tradition the word *sacrament* does not move across all the layers of meaning that we saw in the word *mystery*. It tends to be more restricted to the ritual sense, to Baptism and Eucharist and other major ritual moments. It is not very often used any more, except in technical theological discussion, to describe the other things we found were associated with the word *mystery*; for example, what is hidden in the Cross of Christ or the hidden plan of God.

If the Greek word *mysterion* always etymologically carries a connotation of something hidden and secret, the Latin word *sacramentum* connotes the making holy of some concrete thing. Obviously both words have been useful to Christians in understanding and talking about, among other things, the meal of bread and wine which Jesus commanded to be celebrated in his memory. Yet through nearly twenty centuries of the use of these words, there are naturally shifts in understanding and emphasis, and tracing some of these can be instructive, suggestive of refinements in our own usage.

If we ask what the Church of the first four or five centuries understood about the bread and wine of the Eucharistic rite, we could respond by saying that there was at this time an almost instinctive sense of the nature of a sacrament. The bread and wine was a *sacrament* of the Lord's Body and Blood. (Other terms were also used: *figure* of his Body and Blood, *type* of, *image* of, the *mystery* of . . . , etc.) That is, by means of bread and wine we come into contact with something that now would otherwise be beyond reach; namely, the risen and glorified Body of Christ, no longer confined to space and time. So, by means of a sacrament we come into contact in space and time with

something that transcends space and time. The sacrament is a middle
term between us and the transcendent body of the Lord. I can touch
and hold another person in my hands, make contact with another
through touch. It is not quite the same with Christ, though it is similar. With Christ I touch the *sacrament* of his Body and thereby make
contact with his Body through my body. The sacramental experience
is at one and the same time concrete and transcendent, just as Christ
is concrete and transcendent.

The delicacy and precision of this kind of thinking was in part lost
in the Latin West during the early Middle Ages. In the ninth century,
complicated controversies about how to understand the presence of
Christ in the Eucharist swung between two poles. Was Christ to be
understood as being truly present *(in veritate)* or only symbolically
present *(in figura)*? These poles could not have been considered oppo-
sites in the early Church, where symbolic presence—presence by
means of a sacrament—was not a less real presence, but one appropri-
ate to both the transcendent and concrete reality of Christ. Now, in
these controversies, a symbolic presence seemed to mean a less real,
a less concrete presence. The alternatives hardened into extreme posi-
tions, on the one hand describing the presence of Christ in crudely
realistic terms, on the other hand describing it as a presence not
belonging to the physical world but something entirely symbolic and
spiritual. Neither of these alternatives is correct, though each carries
a partial truth. It took several centuries to establish the view that the
Eucharist can be real without being crudely realistic, and symbolic
without being unreal.

I said in the introduction that paradoxically, to go more deeply
into the meaning of the Mass, we must remain also always on the
surface, never leaving behind its actual forms, for the very forms
themselves—the bread, the wine, the movements of the people—
become completely imbued with significance, with divine life itself.
This is the *sacramental* perspective. The forms are not "merely" or

"weakly" symbolic. They are at one and the same time concrete and transcendent.

The Assembly

Mass begins long before it begins. Much has gone into its preparation, and the actual beginning of the liturgical ceremony is a culmination of many graces mysteriously at work in the lives of hundreds and even thousands of people. Actually we could say that Mass begins with the creation of the world. God intended this kind of encounter with His creatures from the start. I do not have in mind here to trace the beginnings back that far, but I do want at least to suggest such a meditation to my reader. The creation of the world and the history of the human race is the largest context for Mass, and this context is in fact presupposed and expressed in many of the rituals and texts. We will see that as we go through the Mass. But for our purposes now it is perhaps enough to suggest all this and to zero in more closely to what goes into the immediate preparation of a given celebration of Mass. I am not talking about turning on the lights of the building and opening the doors, preparing the vessels and vestments, and getting the music sorted out. I am talking about the deep theological significance hidden in the arrival of many people coming from many places into one place to celebrate the Eucharist. I am talking about the *mystery* of the assembly.

The Mass begins as an assembly forms, and this is already full of meaning. We should notice it, ponder it with wonder, and rejoice in it. In the coming together of many people into one place to pray under the headship of their bishop or a priest, we have an acting out in a very concrete way of what the Church is and is meant to be. The Greek word for *church* is *ekklesia,* and Latin takes this Greek word and uses it as its own. From Latin it passes into the Romance languages. Unfortunately our English word is of a different derivation, and so we have to stretch a little to be sure we hear all that is implied in calling this group an *ekklesia*. Literally in Greek it means "a calling out" and "a calling together." So, *church* means those called out from somewhere by God and called together into one place by Him. Every time we use the word *church* we should try to remember this sense of the word. The Church is the gathering of those called by God; she is an assembly that God forms and keeps together.

So, people just coming to the church building is already a mystery. A divine reality is hidden in their concrete coming. We do well to turn a contemplative gaze to the concrete nature of all that is involved in a community assembling for this celebration. Behind every one of the baptized who has come to celebrate Eucharist stands a magnificent personal story of grace, of struggle and labor and rejoicing, and of all these united around that person's faith. All have received their faith through others who have believed before them and have passed it on. This is *being* Church, and the passing on of faith has this celebration as its ultimate point of arrival. From hundreds of directions involving thousands of persons, faith brings many believers together into one place. This gathering of many people into one place has a specific scope. This people disposes itself for undergoing a divine action. The many will be made one, not through some means of their own devising but by receiving from Christ himself that life which he receives from another, from his eternal Father. It is by receiving from the Lord what they themselves do not have and could never generate that these many who are gathered are brought into a unity which has divine origins. Again, the name for this unity is Church, the assembly of those whom God has called out.

In the Eucharistic celebration itself, many elements express the divine nature of the reality that is occurring; indeed, these elements are the very means of embodying and ensuring the particular and precise nature of what is happening; namely, that Christ is acting and that the community is entirely defined and comes into being only through what he does and accomplishes. Thus, for example, in the person of the bishop or priest Christ is represented as the head of this assembly. It is he who gathers it; it is under his authority that it stands; it is his word that is gratefully heard and pondered; it is together with him that the community will dare to speak a word back to the Father and make its thanksgiving offering to Him.

All this happens in a particular time and place. That time and place are also significant for understanding the mystery of the Church, for in the Eucharist the one time and place of a particular gathering — concretely existing in a specific culture and in a precise moment in history with all the life stories of those who have come together — are expanded and dilated and are made to contain in this particular form the mystery of the universal Church across the world and across the centuries and across the heavens extending to the community of saints and angels in heaven. In any one gathering of a community to celebrate Eucharist, this whole reality of Church is expressed in the signs of the liturgy and is brought into being. The Church is local and located in time, or it cannot come to be. But the local reality is always more than the sum of its parts. The local reality is an icon in which the reality of the universal Church is rendered present. It is for this reason that in the Eucharistic Prayer the local bishop is named, as is the bishop of Rome, with whom the local bishop and bishops across the world verify their communion and apostolic faith. The saints in heaven are named, and the dead are remembered. The year of the celebration is etched boldly on the Easter candle which dominates the sanctuary. All this is contained in the language and cultural forms of the particular place.

So, who is assembled for any given celebration of the Mass? At first glance, we see only a concrete group of given people whose own particular stories have brought them. But hidden in the mystery of this concrete assembly is a much bigger assembly, and the very celebration will reveal the bigger assembly. The whole Church has gathered; the Church in heaven and on earth, the Church across the world and across the centuries. And in that Church is gathered the whole creation and the desires of every human heart. The Mass prepared from the beginning of the world is about to begin. The meaning of the whole creation and the whole of human history is contained here in ritual form and in the people who enact the ritual. This action will cause the Church to be: to do Eucharist is to be Church. To be Church, to be assembled into one, is what God intends for the world. The Eucharist is celebrated in thanksgiving and for the glory of God, and it is done for the salvation of the whole world.

The Overarching Shape of the Entire Rite

The broad strokes of what happens at Mass can be traced in two basic movements which define its essential form, the basic melody line, as it were. The first is a movement from God the Father to the world, while the second is a movement from the world to God the Father. At any given point in the rite we will want to understand in which of these two directions the words and actions are moving. However, these two directions unfold in both a Trinitarian and an ecclesial shape that need to be described in order to hear the fullest resonance of what is moving.

The first movement in this full Trinitarian and ecclesial shape can be described as follows: the Father gives Himself through the Son in the Holy Spirit. It is necessary to pause and to try carefully to grasp the depth and mystery of what this means. Without attention to this dimension of the Eucharist, such Trinitarian formulations are perhaps just pious and habitually uttered phrases. Yet what we are dealing with here is the form, the dynamic, the very shape of God's saving activity on our behalf; namely, that God the Father gives Himself to the world by giving His Son. This is "the Father who so loved the world that he gave His only Son" (John 3:16). But there is more. This direction of movement in the liturgy reveals that the Father gives His Son in and

by the Holy Spirit who is Spirit of the Father. The Father gives His Spirit
an assignment, as it were; namely, to effect and illumine and clarify
and arrange everything in such a way that the Son be known and that
all who believe in him might live their lives entirely from the Son's life.
It is this precise Trinitarian form that is revealed in what happens at
Mass; that is, not merely or vaguely that the Father gives Himself to
the world; but concretely and specifically that the Father gives Himself
to the world in the giving of His Son, a Son at every moment accompanied by the action and work of the Holy Spirit.

Yet, it is possible to be more concrete still. There is another dimension that is constitutive of the shape of this saving activity of God. It
is the Church; that is, concretely the actual gathered assembly to whom
the Father's Son is actually given. The Father does not just merely or
vaguely give His Son to the world, but He does so precisely in and
through the Church. Naturally, I am speaking of where the fullness
of the Father's gift is given, received, and verified. Of course, it is possible to see the action, the grace, the face of Christ in many situations
in the world that appear to have no connection at all or only a very
distant connection with either the Church conceived as institution or
the Church conceived as Eucharistic assembly. Yet the Church that
celebrates Eucharist knows that her mission is to bring everyone and
indeed everything to the Eucharistic table as a gift to be presented for
transformation. This is the mission of the Church because "this being
brought to the altar" is what has been revealed as the will of the Father
for all. (As in 1 Timothy 2:5: "God wants all to be saved and to come
to know the truth.") So even in situations far from the institutional
Church and far from the Eucharistic assembly, the community that
celebrates Eucharist knows precisely from the celebration itself that
all matter and all history have received in Christ a future which is
nothing less than a share in his victory over sin and death. Thus, there
is a dynamic secretly at work in the world which we may call a dynamic
toward Eucharist. Everything and everybody in the world is destined

by grace for Eucharistic transformation. In this way then, we must say that the Father gives His Son to the world through the Church.

An opposite direction also forms part of the basic movement of every Eucharistic celebration; namely, that of the world toward the Father. This too has a Trinitarian and ecclesial shape. When the Father places His Son into the hands of the Church (the first movement), He does so in order that the Church may do something with this gift; namely, offer it as its own back to the Father (the second movement). Or the same mystery can be described from a different angle. When the Word assumes our flesh—this is the form in which the Father gives His Son to us—He does so in order that he may offer it to the Father as what he is and has always been. All this is accomplished in the Holy Spirit. The Spirit who molded a Body for the Word in the womb of the Virgin Mary, the Spirit who raised the Body of Jesus from the dead— this same Spirit now fills the gifts that the Church brings for transformation and makes them to be one same thing: the Body formed from Mary's body, the Body raised from the dead, Christ's body the Church offered to God the Father in the name of the whole world. The world's passing over to the Father in this way can take place *only* in the Church.

I mentioned in the introduction that describing the overarching shape or movement of the Eucharistic rite would unexpectedly require our having to speak of the Trinitarian mystery. In fact, we have seen not only that, but also that it is not possible to speak of the Trinity in the abstract but only in relation to the Church. And the Church exists not for herself but for the sake of the world. So we have named Father, Son, and Spirit in describing the twofold movement of the Eucharistic liturgy, but it has not been possible to do so without also naming Church and world.

THE IDEAL CELEBRATION

In order to think well on a theological level about the Mass, we need to imagine an ideal celebration of the liturgy and not get tangled up in questions of a practical nature concerning how well or how poorly a particular celebration happens. If we have had bad experiences of liturgical celebration, where the ritual is performed poorly or not as envisioned by the Church, we should set that aside at present and imagine the liturgy as it is meant to be celebrated, with every person and every part working at the highest level. Questions of a practical order are, of course, critically important; but that is not our task here. Problematic liturgies that have been poorly celebrated, even when that is the dominant experience of a person's encounter with the Mass, are not the basis on which good theological reflection can be built. This can only be built on envisioning the liturgy ideally celebrated, which the Church's liturgical books articulate and which the best tradition of the Church has maintained. If we can deepen our understanding based on this, we will be more prepared to face practical questions of celebrating in concrete situations. We will recognize problems and know how to solve them.

Again, in order to have a good, fully developed basis on which to ground our reflections, it is helpful to imagine a "big" liturgy; that is, a Sunday or even a major feast, where a large number of people has assembled for the celebration. The celebration of the Sunday Eucharist is normative for Catholic life. It is presumed that everybody in the community will be there. Such a celebration is different from a weekday celebration of the Mass. Of course, on the deepest level what happens at every Mass is the same, and what we say here about the Mass will apply to every celebration, big or small, poorly or well celebrated. Even so, a weekday Mass is not a norm. It is a rich bonus for those for whom such celebrations are possible. But in order to conduct this theological reflection, it will help to be able to refer to a celebration with all its dimensions developed as in a Sunday or a major feast. From the beginning, Sunday has been the preeminent day for Christians to gather together in prayer, since on Sunday Christ rose from the dead, and every Sunday celebrates his Resurrection by the celebration of Eucharist. That celebration inevitably marks the whole day, making Sunday a day completely given over to prayer, to rest in God, to the joy of our communion with one another, to the joy of our salvation. This is the ideal, and we should protect it from cultural encroachments and lifestyles that undermine such a sense of Sunday.

In some sense our imagining this ideal celebration should include the bishop as the one who presides at the liturgy. I know that for the most part the ordinary experience of those who celebrate Mass is with a priest presiding, not the bishop. But behind every priest we need to see the bishop who has ordained him and sent him to a particular community to lead the Eucharistic celebration. (As a reminder of this, when I speak in what follows about the priest's role, I will sometimes refer simply to the priest but other times to the bishop.) In what God has arranged for His people, there is really only one priest, Christ himself. Those whom we call bishops and priests represent the one and only priest, Christ himself. They are mysteries or sacraments; that is, concrete people in whom a divine reality is hidden. In this case they are the reality of Christ as priest.

The bishop is head of a diocesan church; he is its leader and its chief authority. But he is not this as an individual person, the lucky guy who gets to be in charge. He represents Christ as head, Christ the leader, Christ the community's only authority. The source and summit of the life of the diocesan community is the celebration of the Eucharist. And just as there is only one priest, Christ himself, there is also only one Eucharist, the Eucharist that Christ himself as head of his body the Church continually offers together with his Church. This one Eucharist, as we have seen, extends across the centuries and across the whole world; it extends between heaven and earth. The many celebrations of the Mass that occur in many places and all through the

centuries are sacraments of the one Eucharist; that is, concrete somethings in which the one Eucharist is encountered. In the same way, the
many bishops across the world, precisely because they are in communion with each other, teaching the same faith and celebrating the
same Eucharist, are sacraments of the one and only priest who leads
the community's Eucharist, Christ himself.

Likewise then, a priest is not a freefloating agent, the lucky guy
who gets to be in charge in a parish setting. He represents his bishop,
who represents Christ as head of the community. The many priests of
a diocese, precisely because they are in communion with their bishop,
teaching the same faith and celebrating the one and only Eucharist,
are also sacraments of the one and only priest who leads the community's Eucharist, Christ himself. This is called by an ancient tradition
"holy order." Holy Orders is one of the seven sacraments of the Church.
It is this order of communion between a priest and his bishop, between
one bishop and all the rest, that ensures that a given community's
celebration of the Eucharist is not a celebration of its own invention
and manufactured by itself. This is the one and only Eucharist at which
the one and only priest, Jesus Christ, presides.

It is important to remember, however, that Christ shares his priesthood with all the baptized. If the bishop or priest at the head of the
Eucharistic assembly is meant to be a sign of the one priesthood of
Christ, all his words and actions during the rite are geared toward
uniting the people with him in what he is doing. That is, Christ's priesthood exists for the sake of his people. Precisely in the Mass Christ
wishes to unite all his people with himself in his priestly act of offering
himself to the Father for the sake of the world. In this sense all of
Christ's people are priests, not because they represent his one and only
priesthood as bishops and priests do, but because they are united with
him in his priestly act. This is as the apostle Peter exclaims to the
Christians to whom he writes: "You are living stones for the construc-
tion of a spiritual edifice, a holy priesthood, to offer spiritual sacrifices

pleasing to God through Jesus Christ . . . .You are a chosen race, a royal priesthood, a holy nation . . . " (1 Peter 2:5, 9).

* * *

Now we are ready to turn to the celebration itself, beginning at the beginning and walking all the way through. As we do so, let us remember that all that is said and done in this rite is a mystery, a sacrament. It is the manifestation through a particular assembly of the whole mystery of the Church. In the Church the Father gives His Son in the Spirit to the world, and the world through the Church responds in thanksgiving to the Father in Christ and in the Holy Spirit.

Chapter Two

The Introductory Rites

This chapter will be comparatively brief, like the Introductory Rites themselves. I will treat in turn the Entrance Chant, the Sign of the Cross, the Greeting, the Penitential Act, the *Gloria*, and the Collect.

Entrance Chant

The assembly that God has called together rises to its feet and begins to sing. The beauty of song is not insignificant for understanding what is happening. It bespeaks the beauty of the one faith in the many Christians throughout the world. Song expresses the unity of the faith of the assembly in its various parts. Many voices together make one beautiful sound, a poly-phony, a sym-phony. Imagine the cacophony that would be created if all the persons present suddenly began to speak their own words to God with their own various voices. Every voice with its own unique timbre and qualities and way of expression would be swallowed up in the chaos of sound created by the differences of others. But in song all the different qualities of voices and expression blend into one beautiful sound and one beautiful voice. This is the voice of the Church! It is a sounding, an incarnation of the unity of faith, of intercession, of praise from the one Church poised to celebrate the one Eucharist.

Song is a mystery. There is something hidden in the singing of this particular community. This song echoes the hymn sung eternally in the halls of heaven. In fact, hundreds of thousands are singing and countless angels too. The biblical book of Revelation shows us in vision

17

what is hidden in the little assembly of our particular singing. In the vision of the heavenly assembly "there was the Lamb standing on Mount Zion, and with him a hundred and forty-four thousand who had his name and his Father's name written on their foreheads" (Revelation 14:1). All these are singing a "new song" (Revelation 14:3). It is the human race singing now that same song of love that has moved among Father, Son, and Spirit from all eternity. What is new is that others join the Trinitarian rhythms. This is nothing that human beings could arrogate to themselves; it is not the world's song. "No one could learn this song except the hundred and forty-four thousand who had been ransomed from the earth" (Revelation 14:3). Compared with these magnificent visions given to the apostle John, our earthly assemblies for the Eucharist appear at first glance disappointingly humble. But the apostolic visions are given to us precisely so that we can penetrate to the deepest reality hidden in our assemblies.

While the song is being sung, a procession of the various ministers of the liturgy moves through the church and into the sanctuary. At the culminating point of this procession is the bishop or priest, rendering visible and concrete for us what our fleshly eyes cannot see; namely, Christ himself as the head of our assembly and the one who leads us in prayer. This procession acts out and actually causes to happen what it signifies. Christ is coming and standing in the midst of his people. Of course the people rise to their feet! Of course they are singing a joyful song with one voice!

Other ministers accompany the priest in the procession, all dressed in special and different robes signifying the difference in their roles. Some carry flame, another carries the smoking incense. But the liturgy is always more than the sum of its concrete parts. When flame and incense enter, the heavenly choirs of angels enter the sanctuary with them; and they will help us to worship. They will pray for us and with us. They will protect us because they love us. In the procession the deacon carries the Book of the Gospels. This shows us that Christ is coming together with his word. In what is about to happen, he will speak—words of power and wisdom, a transforming word that will change our lives and form us into the likeness of himself. The Book of the Gospels will be placed on the altar in the same place where the holy gifts of bread and wine will later appear. So we see from the start the inseparability of the food of the Word and the food of the Lord's Body and Blood. We see that all the scriptures culminate in the sacrifice that will lie on the altar.

While the assembly is still singing, the priest circles the altar with incense as a sign of reverencing the holy table around which and on which all that is about to happen is concentrated. Again, the book of Revelation helps us to peer through to the heavenly reality: "Another angel came and stood at the altar, holding a gold censer. He was given a great quantity of incense to offer, along with the prayers of all the holy ones, on the gold altar that was before the throne. The smoke of the incense along with the prayers of the holy ones went up before God from the hand of the angel" (Revelation 8:3–4). The sight of the incense and the mysterious atmosphere it creates, its sweet and unusual smell, as well as the glad song that still continues—all of this helps us to take the measure of the place where we now stand and the event that is about to happen. The altar is nothing less than the throne of God and of the Lamb.

"After this I saw before me a huge crowd which no one could count from every nation and race, people and tongue. They stood before the throne of the Lamb, dressed in long white robes and holding palm branches in their hands. They cried out in a loud voice, 'Salvation is from our God, who is seated on the throne, and from the Lamb!' All the angels who were standing around the throne and the elders and the four living creatures fell down before the throne to worship God. They said: 'Amen! Praise and glory, wisdom and thanksgiving and honor, power and might to our God forever and ever. Amen!'" (Revelation 7:9–12)

The human capacity to sing is truly wonderful. Dogs, horses, cows—none of these animals sing. These may make their own sounds, sure enough, but they never achieve what is achieved by human song. Human song is an image of the mystery of the Incarnation. Air in a body, in a throat, pushing the intelligible voice outward in beautiful expression is an image of Spirit in the flesh, of divinity joined to humanity. It is magnificent and well expressive of our emotion. The beauty of our assembly, the beauty of our emotion, comes from Christ who has joined his divinity to our flesh so that he may lead his body in the song of thanksgiving to his Father. Rightly did Saint Augustine exclaim, "To sing is to pray twice."

THE SIGN OF THE CROSS

After the song is ended and all are gathered in their places, the first thing the priest does and says is the Sign of the Cross, signing his body with the cross and saying the words "In the name of the Father, and of the Son, and of the Holy Spirit." All the people likewise sign themselves and answer, "Amen." A more solemn and meaningful beginning cannot be imagined. Let us first think about the sign itself, then the words, then the sign and words used in this context to open the entire rite.

The sign expresses in one summary gesture the central event of Christian faith. We trace it over our own bodies as a way of indicating that that event shall make its force felt on our very bodies. The Body that was crucified on the Cross touches my body and shapes it now for what is about to happen. When we mark this sign on ourselves, we are so accustomed to saying the words "In the name of the Father, and of the Son, and of the Holy Spirit" that we perhaps fail to notice that a considerable distance has been covered between the actual historical Death of Jesus on the Cross and the solemn pronunciation of the name of God as Father, Son, and Holy Spirit. But in fact the mystery of the

Holy Trinity is revealed in the Death of Jesus on the Cross. As we move through the Mass, we will see more in detail how this is so. It is enough for us to notice now that here at the very beginning of the Mass we make a gesture and say words that summarize all that is about to happen. Our own bodies will be drawn into the Body that hung on the Cross, and this sharing in the Death of Christ is the revelation of the Trinitarian mystery.

The phrase "in the name of the Father, and of the Son, and of the Holy Spirit" comes from the risen Lord himself who commanded his 11 disciples to make disciples of all the nations, baptizing them "in the name of the Father, and of the Son, and of the Holy Spirit." He adds the promise, "And know that I am with you always, until the end of the world" (Matthew 28:19–20). Naturally, then, the phrase is precious to the Christian community. It is the verbal formula with which a person is baptized. It always implicitly echoes the Lord's promise to remain with us always. As the centuries advanced and Christians continued to reflect on the tremendous mystery hidden in this deceptively simple formula, some theologians could not help but marvel at and enjoy the paradox of the word *name* in the singular and the three names Father, Son, and Holy Spirit. The one God has only one name, but that name is Father, Son, and Holy Spirit. This is the full name of God. Other names are shorthand for this or say it by implication.

"In the name" could perhaps be more accurately put as "into the name." To baptize literally means to dunk or to plunge. Thus, the Christian is plunged into the name of God in Baptism. It is a sacrament, a mystery, a concrete something. By means of it we are plunged into the very life of God, and this life is Father, Son, and Holy Spirit— a Father who begets a Son, a Son who yields utterly to the Father, a Spirit who from their love proceeds. Into this exchange every Christian is plunged at Baptism. There is nothing abstract about this. For Baptism is also the sacramental plunge into the Death and Resurrection of Christ. To go down into the water is the mystery of dying and being buried with him. To come up from the water is the mystery of rising with him. So, as in the gesture itself, we have again the Cross and the Trinitarian name of God. The rest of the Christian life is a living out of the consequences of the baptismal plunge and an ever deepening entry into this divine mystery. Every time we mark the sign of the cross on our bodies and pronounce at the same time the holy name of God—Father, Son, and Holy Spirit—we are reminding ourselves of our Baptism and choosing it again in our lives.

To place this sign and the holy name of God at the beginning of the Mass is actually the only possible way to begin. The only door through which to enter what is happening is Baptism; that is, our share in the Death and Resurrection of Christ, our share in the divine name Father, Son, and Holy Spirit. What we are about to experience is a deepening of what was begun in us at Baptism, its ratification and its culmination. How disappointing it is then when a priest, against all the rubrics of what is required at this moment, begins with some other words. Anything else will be banal by comparison. This is not just any gathering that is underway. It is nothing less than Christian Baptism brought to its fullest pitch.

The bishop says the words given to us by our risen Lord. All the people say, "Amen." It is worth pausing for a moment on the significance of this word, for it will be said again and again by the people throughout the course of the Mass, and it ought not to be a throwaway phrase. It is a huge word, and to pronounce it is a grace and privilege that should not be taken for granted. It is a Hebrew word and means that what has been said is certain and firmly established. But it means also personally to involve the one saying it. I put my life on the line in what I say Amen to. I agree to it. I ratify it. To say Amen at the beginning of Mass to the name of Father, Son, and Holy Spirit and to the sign of the cross is to say: Yes, I know this is the only way into Eucharist; Yes, I accept again my Baptism; Yes, I believe in the holy name of God, Father, Son, and Holy Spirit. Something similar applies to all the other times we will say Amen throughout the Mass. It means I agree and I am glad for this glorious truth.

Greeting the Assembled People

Then the priest greets the people with one of several possible ritual phrases: "The Lord be with you," or more elaborately, "Grace to you and peace from God our Father / and the Lord Jesus Christ." All the people greet the priest in return, saying, "And with your spirit." These are not meant to be the exchanges of what might occur between just any large group gathered and one who stands up in front with something to say to everyone and so begins with a "Good morning" or "Good evening," as the case may be. This is an exchange uniquely belonging to the Christian community and peculiar to this moment in the community's life when it begins to celebrate the source and summit of its life. It is an exchange that immediately acknowledges the roles that will be played in this ritual action. The priest greets the people not as an individual, some friendly person whom they may or may not know especially well. He greets them in his sacramental role of representing Christ at the head of his body, as Christ who will lead his body in prayer. And he speaks to the people not merely as one may speak to a group gathered whom he may or may not know especially well. He recognizes in them the assembly that God has called together. He sees them as an assembly of baptized people who are poised for the great sacrifice and act of worship to which their Baptism has admitted them. He spreads his arms wide as he speaks in a stylized gesture of gracious openness. It is the Lord himself whom we are meant to see and hear in this unusual gesture, spoken in unusual language from a man dressed in unusual clothes.

These words come from greetings which the apostle Paul used in his letters. I have said a number of times that the bishop and priest represent Christ at the head of his community. Actually they do this by representing the apostles to whom Christ passed on his mission and authority before being taken from their sight. The apostles for their part passed this on to their successors, the bishops; and bishops share their apostolic ministry of leadership with priests. The greeting of the liturgy is meant to express all this, and so no other kind of greeting will do. With this greeting we are reminded that the faith in which we stand comes to us from the apostles. Immediately we feel our community with them and with the saints who through generations of faithfulness have carried the apostolic faith to our times. With one of these formulas the priest is actually addressing the people with a greeting from God Himself, coming to us through Christ Jesus. It is a way of immediately lifting the assembly up to that level which I have described as exceeding the sum of the parts.

If the priest's greeting to the people is on such an exalted level, the people's response is no less highly pitched. They answer, "And with your spirit." This response, unusual and strange as a formulation and from the earliest centuries needing explanation, is not meant to say something to the effect of "the same to you." It means much more. The people are addressing the "spirit" of the priest; that is, that deepest interior part of his being where he has been ordained precisely to lead the people in this sacred action. They are saying in effect, "Be the priest for us now," aware that there is only one priest, Christ himself, and that this one who represents him now must be finely tuned to perform his sacred duties well.

Only in the tones of the dignified courtesy of this exchange between priest and people can we begin this liturgy, for the exchange expresses and establishes the unique harmony between ourselves, our bishop (or the bishop's priest) as successor of the apostles, and the Church throughout the world, which holds the faith that comes to us from the apostles.

THE PENITENTIAL ACT

Next, the priest urges the people to acknowledge their sins, including himself in the admonition. The basic reason for this, right here at the beginning, is, as one of the suggested texts he may use states, to "prepare ourselves to celebrate these sacred mysteries." The sacred action that is beginning inevitably awakens in us a keen sense of how our sins stand in striking contrast to what we are about to do. We are in the presence of the all holy God, and as a first reaction to finding ourselves there, what can we do except beg Him for His mercy? What could we ever hope to understand of the inspired word of God that is about to be read if we did not confess our sins before God and beg Him for His mercy? How could we ever hope to enter into communion with the sacrifice of Christ if we were to approach it as something to which we had a right? No, we draw near to the word, we draw near to the altar with repentance.

There are different formulas that the priest may use for this part of the rite. They are striking. In one of these we all pray together the Confiteor. What is beautiful in this prayer is that in it we not only confess our sins to God but also to one another, "to you, my brothers and sisters." And then—also a beautiful move—we ask Mary and all the angels and saints and again one another "to pray for me to the Lord our God." By so praying we are immediately brought into an awareness that the liturgy is not about just me and God. All of us together come into His presence, together with angels and saints; and we ask Him to show us His mercy and grant us His salvation. It bears repeating, insistence, even a kind of stammering: "Lord, have mercy. / Lord, have mercy. / Christ, have mercy. / Christ, have mercy. / Lord, have mercy. / Lord, have mercy."

THE *GLORIA*

With the *Gloria* we come to the first element in the Mass that is not always a part of every celebration. The *Gloria* is sung on the big days, on Sundays and the feasts, though not on the Sundays of Advent and Lent. (In Advent and Lent we abstain from singing this hymn so that it can ring out with fresh vigor on the feasts for which these seasons prepare us.) It is an angelic song, beginning with the words the angels sang to the shepherds on the night Christ was born: "Glory to God in the highest / and on earth peace to people of good will" (see Luke 2:14). By using the angels' same words we know that we are singing with them now, or we could just as well say it in the other direction: they are singing with us. We are singing now for the same reason that the angels first sang; namely, that God has sent His Son among us born in our same flesh. Humble and lowly he comes among us, and so, struck with awe at this unexpected shape of the divine plan, as the angels themselves were, we cry out in a hymn to God's glory.

In the first part of the song our words are addressed to God the Father. The language of praise and adoration is insistent: "We praise you, / we bless you, / we adore you, / we glorify you, / we give you thanks for your great glory." Then we turn to address Jesus Christ himself, acknowledging him first as "Only Begotten Son of the Father." Then we cry out to him: "Lord God, Lamb of God, Son of the Father, / you take away the sins of the world," and so in the midst of our praise we beg him again for mercy. This is as we have just seen in the confession of our sins. In the presence of the all holy God, we must beg for mercy. To Jesus, from whom we ask mercy, we say, "you alone are the Holy One, / you alone are the Lord, / you alone are the Most High." This hymn, this shout, concludes by exulting again in the triune name of God: "Jesus Christ, / with the Holy Spirit, / in the glory of God the Father."

This hymn, on the days when it is sung, is an outburst of joy and praise. The liturgy is on the verge of beginning its first major part in the Liturgy of the Word, but it is as if we can hardly get started because of the joy and wonder of Sunday or the feast. So we stand there singing this explosive hymn even though we know God is wanting to address us in His word, and, of course, we are anxious for that. But first, this praise! First, all these names for God the Father and for the Son who is seated at His right hand!

THE COLLECT

Perhaps the term Collect is strange to our ears, but what it expresses helps us to understand well this moment. The priest solemnly invites the people, "Let us pray." Of course, we have been praying from the start, so this invitation means to signal a shift of levels, prayer with a different kind of attention. After a short pause for silence, the priest stretches out his hands and says a prayer whose purpose is to *collect*, into a few short lines, all the strands of what has taken place so far, as well as all the strands of our many individual thoughts, which come from many directions and stray in many directions here at the beginning of our prayer. So this Collect effectively places us all together into one succinctly expressed address to God the Father.

The prayer is addressed to Him and is always structured according to the same pattern, according to a very ancient usage. It helps to be attentive and listen for this pattern. God is first addressed, using one or more of His many titles. Thus, "Almighty ever-living God," or something similar. Next we *remember* before God what God has done—certainly not because He has forgotten, but because *remembering* is from biblical times a fundamental form of prayer. It is our way of acknowledging what He has done on our behalf. Next, on the basis of what is remembered, we ask for something in the present, for ourselves and for the whole Church and world, which is assembled in our assembling. When we remember what God has done in the past, we have courage and reason to hope for what we ask for in the present. If it is a feast, what we remember before God in the prayer is the particular saving event that is the subject of the feast. Something similar is awakened in the liturgical seasons. On Sundays in Ordinary Time, some more generally formulated saving action of God is recalled, but it is always an event remembered that becomes the basis for petition.

In the final move of this pattern of prayer, all that we ask the Father is asked "Through our Lord Jesus Christ, your Son, / who lives and reigns with you in the unity of the Holy Spirit, / one God, forever and ever." Once again we see the threefold name of God, but a little more has happened here than what we saw in the sign of the cross, where the names are simply lined up in a row: Father, Son, and Holy Spirit. In the pattern of the Collect, we have the shape or pattern of prayer that will mark all the praying of the Mass. All the prayers are addressed *to* God the Father, *through* the Son, *in* the Holy Spirit. This is the shape of our prayer; this is the pattern of our movement within the divine life of the Trinity. To this prayer all the people say, "Amen." As mentioned earlier, we will say this word a number of times. Each time our hearts and minds and bodies and souls should be behind the word that sounds from our tongue. We say Amen to our being collected into one to speak to the Father, through the Son, in the Holy Spirit.

Chapter Three

The Liturgy of the Word

Now begins the first major part of the liturgy: the Liturgy of the Word. Our reflection will begin with some general remarks about what happens in the liturgy when the Word of God is proclaimed. We will try to understand what it means to say that God speaks. Then we will discuss what can be called the event character of the proclamation of the Word. What this means will become clear in due time. After these general remarks, we will look at the significance of the full range of readings that we have at Sunday Eucharist or at the Eucharist of a major feast; namely, a First Reading from the Old Testament, a Responsorial Psalm, a Second Reading from the apostolic letters of the New Testament, the Verse before the Gospel, and the Gospel. After this there follows, still considered a part of this first major part of the liturgy, a homily, the Creed, and the Universal Prayer.

What Does it Mean to Say "God Speaks"?

In order to understand well what is happening during the Liturgy of the Word, we will want to remember what was said in chapter one about the overarching shape of the liturgy. We spoke there of a twofold movement: a movement of God toward the world and of the world toward God. In this part of the liturgy this movement is enacted by means of speech. God speaks, and we respond. If we unfold this into its Trinitarian and ecclesial shape, we can say that God speaks through His Son in the Holy Spirit to the Church; and the Church responds. Christ stands exactly in the middle position of these two directions of movement, and thus he is named Mediator. What God says to the world *is* His Son, Christ. What the world says back to God is also Christ, the Word made flesh. The Church also plays the role of mediator here. God speaks to the world in speaking to the Church. The Church speaks for the world in responding to God.

We need to reflect more precisely on what it means to say that God speaks. This is not as simple as words like our words just coming out of the sky somehow, a little larger and a little louder so that we think, "Oh, that must be God speaking! I wonder what he wants?" No, that God has a word is mysteriously part of His very essence, and He reveals Himself to us as such. "In the beginning was the Word, and the Word was with God, and the Word was God" (John 1:1). God is expression of Himself. He is that from all eternity. "Within" God there is God and His expression. This is Father and Son, God and Word from all eternity. Then God takes His expression and expresses it "outside" Himself, in the creation of a universe. The eternal expression, the eternal Word, is the basis or the principle of creation: "Through him [the Word] all things came into being and apart from him nothing came to be" (John 1:3). What God is is Life itself. "Life" is another name for God and His expression. In the creation God shares His Life outside Himself: "Whatever came to be, in him [the Word] found Life." So, the very creation itself is God speaking. Creation is His expression, and He has placed us within it with a capacity to discern His Word there and respond to it. We are not meant to listen to some loud voice booming down from the sky, but to the very creation itself and to our own selves as a part of it.

The sin of our first parents was a failure to discern this Word and this Life whose origins are in God. It is consequently a refusal to respond and to be in relationship with God who speaks. The legacy of this broken relationship becomes the history of the race that springs from our first parents. Humanity, made to hear the Word of God and respond to it, no longer has ears and no longer knows how to speak a word of response.

Even so, God does not cease to speak. He tries, we could say, other methods of getting through, other methods of expression. In the end, He makes a huge thrust of Himself outward. The divine expression, the Word, goes to unimaginable lengths to get through. "The Word became flesh and made his dwelling among us" (John 1:14). This means that God is expressing Himself no longer merely in the creation but also within the very unfolding of human history. This is remarkable, for in some sense the creation always remained God's pure expression of Himself, and it was human beings who simply no longer knew how to hear it. But as I indicated, human history becomes a history of the race's broken relationship with God, a history where sin and evil accumulate enormous momentum through the rolling centuries. To say, "The Word became flesh and made his dwelling among us" is to say that God is now making His Word to sound within this history of sin, not through the creation alone but by His own acting among us. In the Word made flesh, in Jesus Christ, human beings can hear again who and what God is. We do not hear—I want to say it again—a loud voice booming from the sky. We see this Word. As the text continues, "The Word became flesh and made his dwelling among us, and we have seen his glory, the glory of an only Son coming from the Father, filled with enduring love" (John 1:14). To see the glory of an only Son coming from the Father is to hear God's Word. It is to see and hear who and what God is. God is a Father from whom there comes forth an only Son filled with enduring love.

To careful listeners, what I called the huge thrust of God's Word in the flesh-taking of Jesus Christ was not a word coming out of nowhere. Jesus Christ did not drop from the sky. He came quietly, secretly, mysteriously (!) advancing through the centuries. Only in this way could the Word truly *become* flesh, as opposed to merely taking flesh as his outer garment. In fact the divine Word that finally sounds in the human life of Jesus was a Word slowly being prepared by the "words" of many centuries of human history. With the hindsight that comes from hearing God's definitive word in Jesus Christ, Christians were able to understand that in fact God was already speaking in human history in that He was preparing history for this uttering of His final Word. This is expressed beautifully at the beginning of the letter to the Hebrews: "In times past, God spoke in fragmentary and varied ways to our fathers through the prophets. In this, the final age, he has spoken to us through his Son, whom he has made heir of all things and through whom he first created the universe" (1:1–2).

As the world was approaching this "final age"—final because God can say no more than He has said in Christ—the setting in which the Word will be definitively uttered is focused in the history of Israel. This is the nation sprung from Abraham, to whom Moses was sent as chief actor in the events surrounding the Exodus, to whom the Law and the Prophets were given, within which David was promised a dynasty that would last forever. This was a nation that, despite countless signs of God's special favor and intentions to speak and act through its history, would again and again fall away from Him. Yet God remains faithful to His promises and, as we have said, in this context finally utters His definitive Word.

Now, to return to concepts developed in chapter one, we can say that Jesus Christ is the *mystery* of creation and history. That is, in the concrete something of the created world and in the history of the human race the secret—hidden and now revealed—is Jesus Christ, the eternal Word of God, the only Son coming from the Father filled with enduring love. This—he!—is the Word of God that is proclaimed and celebrated in Mass during the Liturgy of the Word. He is what happens. The Word of God is not a book, is not the Bible as a bunch of words whose meaning we are meant to figure out. The Word of God is the creation, is the history of Israel, is the story of Jesus Christ. Christians are those who have heard and received God's definitive

Word in Jesus Christ. After him, the creation and the earlier history of Israel can only be heard as part of his story. Indeed, the joy of hearing the story of creation and of Israel's history is to see its culmination in Christ. Every detail is garnered and pondered for what it can reveal of him.

THE EVENT CHARACTER OF THE PROCLAMATION OF THE WORD

So, the "Word of God" in the Liturgy of the Word does not mean the words of the Bible considered merely as words like our words. The Word of God *is* an event: the *event* of creation and the *event* of what God is doing and saying in Israel and finally the *event* of what God is doing and saying in Jesus. The words of the Bible narrate the event. They are a precious means to us, for they are given by the Holy Spirit. As such, they carry far more than mere human words can carry. They carry the very events of which they speak, and in their formulation is revealed the mystery of the event. In the proclamation of these words, the event proclaimed becomes present. The words in the book are rather like the notes of a musical score. The score is not the music. But the score lets the music sound. When from the score of the biblical book the words are proclaimed in the midst of a believing assembly, the music of God's events sounds forth in the midst of that assembly! What is the basic shape of the music? God speaks to the world, and the world speaks to God. God "says" His Son to the world, and the world "says" itself as Son back to God.

No matter what particular readings occur in a given liturgy, the Liturgy of the Word always has about it an event character; that is, the events of the past that are proclaimed become event for the believing community that hears them told. And all the events of Sacred Scripture find their center in the one event that is the center of them all: the Death and Resurrection of Jesus. It is this about which all of Sacred

Scripture speaks. This is not talk delivering ideas and concepts. It is, as I say, an event: the same event in which God once acted to save His people delivered now to this assembly by means of the biblical score, the gift of the Spirit to the Church.

Liturgy is an event in the same sense as all other events in the economy of salvation—the intervention of the living God in human history, which, precisely because it is God's doing, cannot slip into the past. In a given liturgy, specific words from Sacred Scripture are proclaimed. The Holy Spirit, who crafted these words through human authors, has placed in them a power, which in every moment allows them to be received anew as an actual communication of salvation. Every proclamation of the Word in the liturgy is an irreducibly new moment: the event of Christ—all the events of Sacred Scripture are the event of Christ—becomes the event of the Church; i.e., of a particular assembly that here and now hears this Word.

The Word proclaimed in liturgy is not some pale reflection or residue of the event proclaimed there. It is the whole reality to which the words bear testimony made present. What was spread out as a series of events through time is now concentrated into the one event of this liturgy.

Such claims about the power of the scriptural words could not be made were it not for the action of the Holy Spirit, whom the risen Lord gives to the Church and whose gift and creation the Sacred Scriptures are, whose inspiration is needed to understand them aright. Put another way, the risen Lord himself must open our minds in the Spirit to the understanding of those words. When he does, our minds grasp nothing less than the wonderful reality that this moment of listening becomes in the very hearing an event of salvation, the same event that the words proclaim.

This is true for us in virtue of Jesus' Resurrection, for his Resurrection does not simply mean that he has somehow been detached from the life he lived and is back again—who knows how—after death. Jesus rose from the dead with the whole life he once lived rising with him. If death means life is over, you're stuck where you die and time goes on without you, then resurrection from the dead means this life lived is not over, not lost, not subject to decay. So it is that every word that Jesus spoke, every action he performed can be present to us because it rose with him. And all that he ever said and did is concentrated in a supreme way in the hour of his dying. And so this event especially is present to us in his Resurrection. But not only that. When we remember that Jesus did not drop from the sky but became flesh through the long centuries of the waiting creation and of Israel's history, then we realize that all of this rises with him as well. Every event of Israel's past is part of the event that he is, and when he rises from the dead and appears now in the midst of our assembly, all those events are part of the one event that he is, and what he is *is* the event of this liturgy.

We can turn now to the form and order of the ritual in which the Word is proclaimed at Mass. All that we have said here is given concrete form by what we read, how we read, who reads, and the order in which we read. This form and order express that the center of what is proclaimed is the Death and Resurrection of Jesus. The spreading out of many scriptural texts throughout the liturgical year repeats in our community's experience and understanding what the Church in each generation discovers with awe and wonder: that the meaning of the whole creation and the whole of human history is revealed in the mystery of the Death and Resurrection of Jesus Christ.

We can begin with an observation about the structure of the Liturgy of the Word. The Sacred Scriptures are read in a certain order, an order that follows the order of salvation history; that is, the liturgy begins with a text from the Old Testament, where creation and the history of Israel are recounted, and moves toward the climax of the proclamation of the Gospel. This is the order of the Liturgy of the Word because the Gospel is the climax and center of Sacred Scripture, or put more comprehensively: because Christ himself is the fulfillment of creation and the history of Israel. Thus, for a Christian, only from the perspective of the Gospel is the Old Testament text understood in its fullness, or again: only in Christ are creation and the history of Israel understood. Some reading from the writings of the apostles forms a link between Gospel and Old Testament, a contemplative insight, a theological insight that helps bind the event of the Gospel to the event of the Old Testament.

I am not speaking here necessarily of specific sets of texts as found in the Lectionary for the celebration of a given day, where this connection is sometimes more, sometimes less clear, as the case may be. The point is a general one about this structure in the liturgy. However, once the theological significance of this structure is grasped—the structure is a mystery!—profound and unexpected connections can emerge between the texts that will not appear when the texts are simply read side by side as texts.

THE OLD TESTAMENT READING

We have said that the Gospel is the center of the Liturgy of the Word. This claim has its roots in the Old Testament, and on a most basic level, it is a careful reading of the text as a whole, which leads us to make such a claim. The Old Testament is a vast collection of theological traditions developed during well over a thousand years. Yet, despite the differences of the many human circumstances and authors that are reflected there, it is not difficult for the one who reads with faith to see that the collection as a whole leads to a center. Everything is organized around the Exodus, the wandering in the desert, the coming into the Promised Land. All things either lead to that, recount that, or look back to that. The whole of revelation for Israel is focused in what God manifested himself to be in these events. Every subsequent generation remembered and celebrated them, defined their present dealings with God in reference to them. Jesus, as a Jewish man, would have done the same. These events, then, become directly part of who he is. He expresses himself in terms of them. This is especially true of the days leading up to his Death and culminating in it.

When a passage from this collection is read at Mass, now in virtue of Jesus' Resurrection, that original event becomes the event of the community that hears it. The Christian community hears it with the insight lent it by the presence of its risen Lord. What happens at Mass in this moment was expressed already in the Gospel of Luke where the story of the risen Lord's appearance to the two disciples along the road to Emmaus is recounted. "'How slow you are to believe all that the prophets have announced! Did not the Messiah have to undergo all this so as to enter into his glory?' Beginning, then, with Moses and all the prophets, Jesus interpreted for them every passage of scripture which referred to him" (Luke 24:27). Or again, as in another appearance: "Jesus said, 'Everything written about me in the law of Moses and the prophets and psalms had to be fulfilled.' Then he opened their minds to the understanding of the scriptures. He said to them: 'Thus it is written that the Messiah must suffer and rise from the dead on the third day'" (Luke 24:44–46). It is the Lord himself who teaches the center of Israel's Scriptures, not as an outside interpreter, but as prophet and Messiah sent to the nation, he himself a part of the nation. And that center is this: that the Messiah—Jesus himself!—must suffer so to enter into glory. Cross and Resurrection.

The community that listens to this Word at Mass is a community of the disciples of Jesus. It knows that by hearing his Word it will be more and more conformed to him. But then this means that the community's story and the story of each individual in it takes on the same shape and pattern that we find in the story of Jesus. We have already heard that shape expressed in summary form: the Messiah must suffer so to enter into glory. So also the disciples of Jesus.

The actual proclamation of the Word during Mass has its own power just in virtue of its being announced, its being pronounced aloud in the believing assembly. The Word penetrates the minds and hearts of all who are present and mysteriously begins to shape each and all together into this pattern of suffering and glory. But we must also actively listen to the Word and ourselves search for the connection between the patterns of our lives and the biblical patterns. In this way we become a community which discovers that the meaning of our personal existence—and indeed, the meaning of the whole world—cannot be understood apart from the great patterns of the sacred text. This means that the Word is ever new. We don't leave our lives and our moment in history behind as we listen to these stories from the past; we actually take them up anew in the light of the Word we have heard. The story of our lives is seen to be part of a larger story—the story that the Bible tells.

Let us take an example that briefly mentions many of the themes (not all) that might be slowly heard during the course of the year as Old Testament texts are read in the liturgy. (I note in italics single words that embody major themes of the text.) In the original *creation* the whole world may be understood to be God's *temple. Sin* destroys our capacity to live in the *world* as in God's *temple*, but the *covenant* with *Abraham* and *Moses* can be viewed as moving toward the building of a temple in *Jerusalem*, where once again God's *presence* in our midst is known and celebrated. But we can only hear these texts thinking of Jesus, and all that they say gives us language and images for thinking of him. Jesus transposes the key in which the *temple* of his day is understood. By his *Death* he mysteriously destroyed it, as he had predicted. And in three days a *new temple,* his risen and glorified *Body* is raised up. But these patterns reach all the way to us now, for as Saint Paul says, we are that *temple* built of living stones.

Finally, we should take into account the one who reads. Who should do this, and how is it best done? More is happening here, or should be, than just a sense of "somebody has to do this," and so we choose one of the baptized. To read in the liturgy is one of the great privileges of our Baptism. Even as we listen to another, we should marvel at the grace that enables one of us to stand up and be used as an instrument through which the holy and life-giving Word of God is announced in the assembly. It is clear then that the more the reader is conscious of this, the more effectively the Word will be proclaimed. The reader's own understanding and faith must appear in the act of reading, the reader's own living of the patterns and realities which the text expresses. In short, holiness of life, and not mere rhetorical technique, makes for effective reading. This does not mean that someone might maintain something to the effect of "I'm holy now, so I'm ready to read" any more than "I'm not holy, so I can't read." It is a question of what we strive for. We hear between the lines of the reading the reader's own struggle in discipleship, and we are encouraged by this in our own.

At the end of the proclamation of the passage, the reader bluntly declares what it is that we have just heard: "The word of the Lord." Though it need not literally be done, this is like a great shout, a trumpet call. The declaration should be heard with absolute amazement. How absurd it would be to take for granted that God should speak in our midst. We are expressing our amazement, and we are saying that we do not take it for granted when we cry out from the depths of our hearts, "Thanks be to God."

THE RESPONSORIAL PSALM

Silence is our initial response to the word we have heard. This is not first of all the silence in which one is meant to *think* hard about what we have just heard, though, of course, it will include that. This is primarily the silence of awe and adoration in the presence of God who has spoken to us. What possible response could we have to what He has said? How pitiable our words would be following on the heels of His. We have said that ultimately the Word spoken by the Father to the Church is Jesus Christ himself. The silence of the assembly at this point is the same about which we read in the heavenly liturgy described in the book of Revelation: "When the Lamb broke open the seventh seal, there was silence in heaven for about thirty minutes" (8:1).

But then this also becomes a silence in which we can be reflective about the particular passage we have heard. By pondering it I grasp the biblical pattern in which I myself am intimately involved, in which we are all together intimately caught up. I pray in my heart my wonder and gratitude and beg mercy for my failings. Christ, my risen Lord, is present to me in the depths of my mind and heart, and he "opens my mind to the understanding of the scriptures" (Luke 24:45). We shall all be able to say, "Were not our hearts burning inside us as he talked to us on the road and explained the scriptures to us?" (Luke 24:32).

In effect, during the silence, God's Word spoken to the community, who is Jesus Christ himself, sinks down into the heart of the assembly. Jesus Christ sinks down into the heart of his Church. If he is the Word spoken by God the Father to the Church, he will now also be the Word made flesh in the heart of this community, uttering a response to the Father. Without him our response would be, as I have said, pitiable. With him it is completely adequate! The Father, of course, awaits our response to Jesus Christ whom he has spoken to us, but we choose Jesus himself as our response. This is as Saint Paul once exclaimed, "Whatever promises God has made have been fulfilled in him; therefore it is through him that we address our Amen to God when we worship together" (2 Corinthians 2:20). What we have heard and grasped in the reading are God's promises fulfilled in Christ. We say Amen to God through him because "he was never anything but Yes" (2 Corinthians 2:19).

We use the words of the psalms for our response. We do so because this was Israel's hymn book and so was the prayer book of Jesus himself in his earthly existence. The psalms were produced and then prayed throughout all the various epochs and phases of Israel's existence. In them are embodied the prayers of a people who heard God speaking in the creation and in the events of her history. They express joy and wonder, gratitude and repentance, pleas for help and mercy and protection. The psalms pray a Spirit-inspired response to the patterns of Israel's history as these patterns take on ever clearer shape and form. But like the rest of the Old Testament texts, with the coming of Jesus Christ, the psalms shift onto a new level of meaning which refers entirely to him and his story as the center of Israel's story. We have already noted that the risen Lord himself said as much: "Everything written about me in the law of Moses and the prophets and psalms had to be fulfilled" (Luke 24:44).

The words written in the psalms were fulfilled by Jesus as he prayed them during the course of his life. Verse by verse, psalm by psalm, they were a mystery, hidden but now revealed in him. With these words he spoke to his Father from his human flesh, from the place in Israel's history in which he lived. As he lived that history and prayed to his Father all the while, in his own name and in the name of his nation, he was absorbing into himself, assuming into himself, the entire history of the nation, and so of the world. All this culminates in what the Law and the Prophets predicted: that the Messiah would suffer and rise again on the third day. In the same way that the psalms were Israel's prayers concerning what the Law and Prophets spoke of, so they were Christ's prayers as he lives out the mystery of what is contained in the Law and Prophets. As Christ dies, the psalms are still on his lips. (See Matthew 27:46; Mark 15:34; Luke 23:46; John 19:28.) When he rises again, his way of praying rises with him and becomes in the liturgy his praying in us. From the beginning he and his Church understood the Resurrection and sang their thanks in the words of the psalms. (See Acts 2:22–37; 13:33; Hebrews 1:4–14, passim.)

We want to be mindful again of the direction of the twofold movement of the liturgy. In the First Reading God speaks to us, and in the Responsorial Psalm we speak to God. Christ is in the middle; he is mediator. Because there is a change of direction between the reading and psalm, in the ideal liturgy on which we are basing our reflection, the cantor of the psalm is a different person from the reader. It is presumed that if at all possible, the psalm will be sung. In any case, the antiphonal style articulates in a lovely way the coordination of the voice of the Church with the voice of Christ. It is he who is speaking when the antiphon is sung the first time, and with him "opening our minds to the understanding of the scriptures" (Luke 24:45) as he does so, we will hear the whole history of Israel gathered in his voice. As the assembly repeats the same words, it is singing with him his song to the Father. Then the assembly listens as he continues in the voice of the cantor with some of the verses. By listening, the assembly lets itself be led in its prayer, led by Christ himself. This is why ideally someone different from the reader leads the psalm. It is more difficult to detect the change of direction in the dialogue between God and His Church when the reader also reads the psalm. When for practical reasons, the reader must also read the psalm, at least the silence between reading and psalm should be carefully observed. The effect is lost if the reader races along through the reading at a high rate of speed and, with no silence in between, starts up the psalm as soon as the reading is over. The rhythm of the words and the spaces of silence help the assembly to enter into the dialogue.

In the same way that I suggested that there is something to marvel at when one of the baptized is able to stand up in the assembly and proclaim the very Word of God in its midst, something similar is true of the voice of the cantor leading the assembly in song. Christ borrows the voice and talent of one of his own members and uses it as his voice of prayer in the midst of his Church. Of course, knowing how to sing is important, or it won't work. But more important still for how it ultimately comes off is the cantor's own understanding of how extraordinary is the mystery of the human voice being lent to the risen Lord for his song.

The Second Reading

Much of what has been said about the reading of the Word of God from the Old Testament can be applied to the Second Reading, always taken from one of the letters of the apostles. As we have seen in Jesus himself, the New Testament authors move within the thought world represented in the Old Testament text. They continue the sort of reading of Sacred Scripture that was already well established there, and they discern in them—in the Exodus, the desert, the promised land, the temple—the foreshadowing and indeed some hint of explanation for the wonderful events that unfolded in the life of Jesus of Nazareth. Jesus becomes a new center for such readers, and the texts of the New Testament are the written evidence of their way of reading the Old.

Jesus may be said to be a new center of the history of Israel, but his own life itself has a center. The Gospels and the apostolic letters lead us clearly toward this center. We have said already what it is: his Death and Resurrection.

If we look at the content of the preaching of the primitive Church as represented in somebody like Saint Paul, we can see a situation that did not yet feel the need of something like the Gospel genre. Paul preached only the Death and Resurrection of Jesus, and he managed to preach the Gospel without reference to the many words, parables, miracles of Jesus, not to mention the details of his birth. In other circumstances and as the years passed, communities felt the need for a more extended narrative of the life of Jesus. From this the four Gospels arise. In the case of Matthew and Luke this need reaches back to the very origins and birth of Jesus. But in every case, whatever was narrated about Jesus—be it the marvelous details surrounding his birth, be it the words and deeds of his active ministry—had as its purpose placing the mystery of his Passion in its fuller context, a center which a preacher like Paul could never let us lose sight of. We will say more about the reading of the Gospel shortly. Here we want to say something about the distinctive quality of the Second Reading and its role in the liturgy.

The direction of movement shifts again. God speaks again to His Church, and the Church listens. But now God's language is no longer the creation and the history of Israel. He speaks to us through the reflective writings of the Lord's chosen apostles. I think of this as a contemplative moment. The apostles provide us with penetrating reflections on the center. This is theology, the reflective effort of the first believers to absorb all that had been experienced in the Death and Resurrection of Jesus. They unfold its consequences, showing in various ways that the believer is summoned to an unimaginably profound sharing in the Lord's Passion and so in his victory. All of this is done with key concepts and many citations from the Old Testament. When the Christian community eventually identifies and establishes a canon of New Testament texts, it is a way of saying that in these texts we recognize the living faith that was passed on to us from the apostles, the eyewitnesses of Jesus' Death and Resurrection. (By implication, other texts that did not become part of the canon were seen not to embody this apostolic faith.) The texts are considered inspired; that is, through them the Holy Spirit leads us to the understanding of Jesus' Death and Resurrection that God intends. So, this is what happens at Mass when the writings of an apostle are proclaimed: the assembly is led in that moment to a grasping of the mystery. This interior understanding is what God is now saying to His people, and the reader declares as much when he or she has finished. As before, the reader says, "The word of the Lord." We express our amazement and gratitude as we respond, "Thanks be to God."

As was the case after the First Reading, our most basic response to this reading is the silence that expresses our reverence for the fact that God has spoken. In this silence once again, in the new content delivered and grasped in this reading, Jesus Christ himself is sinking down into the hearts and minds of his people. He is pleased to do so through the words of his apostles, for he has entrusted all that he is, his entire mission, to them. "As the Father has sent me into the world, so do I send you," the risen Lord says to them on the evening of the day on which he rose (John 20:21; see also 17:18).

It is striking how Jesus makes his whole message depend on the apostles and their faithfulness to what they receive from him. At first glance this can be a little disappointing. After only a brief period in which the risen Lord lets himself be seen, he withdraws definitively from sight, after which everything depends on the apostles who witness his Resurrection. Those who believe, although they have never seen Christ, believe not because they have seen the risen Lord, but because they believe what the apostles witness to. This would be less, not more, were it not for the fact that the apostolic testimony is undergirded by the power of the Holy Spirit, who on the day of Pentecost rushed upon these potentially disappointing figures and made them instead powerful witnesses. We are surprised by what we receive from our encounter with them. We believe what the apostles believed. It all depends on that. And this, unexpectedly, is more — not less. We encounter the risen Lord *through* their witness. In making everything depend on the apostles, our risen Lord is surely teaching us how thoroughly serious he is in his intention to be one body with his Church. He is teaching us that he lives and acts only through her. He does not put in private appearances as risen Lord that would stun the lucky viewers. Instead, he appears in his one, holy, catholic, and apostolic Church.

THE ACCLAMATION BEFORE THE GOSPEL

We do not sing a psalm in response to this Second Reading. Rather, the reading has prepared us for what next will follow; namely, the proclamation of the Gospel as the joyful climax of this entire part of the liturgy. So after the silence we rise to our feet and sing not once but many times the one word most closely associated with the Lord's

Resurrection: Alleluia! It is a shout of praise. It is the Lord's own word as he stands risen from the dead before his Father, and his Spirit makes the same word rise up from his body, the Church. We sing this word now because in the proclamation of the Gospel our risen Lord intensifies his presence in this assembly. We know it; we believe it; we are glad about it; we are on our feet; we are singing. We shall hang on his every word and deed.

Flame and the sweet smell of smoking incense make their appearance again. A procession forms. The bishop from his chair blesses one of the deacons he has ordained and directs him to lift the Book of the Gospels from the altar where it had been placed and to carry it aloft in procession to the place from which the Gospel will be proclaimed. All these are mysteries. Through them the transcendent Lord speaks directly to his Church.

THE PROCLAMATION OF THE GOSPEL

We have said that when Jesus rises from the dead, everything he ever said and did rises with him. By means of the reading of some particular passage from the Gospel text, there is delivered to the community some portion, so to speak, of what has risen with Jesus. But, of course, in actuality there is no portioning now. For if a portion can be delivered, it is only because Jesus is entirely risen. But "risen" is not some abstract concept, some vague presence. The one who actually said and did these things, the one who was crucified and buried—this is the one who is risen. So, to hear any one part of the Gospel on any given day is our way, our entry, that day into the whole mystery of the Resurrection. The Gospel is always about the Death and Resurrection of Jesus. Whatever else it tells has as its purpose placing the mystery of his Passion in its fuller context.

The Gospels, too, are apostolic texts, and so all that we have just said about the faith that comes to us through the apostles applies also to our listening to and accepting what we hear in the Gospel reading. The difference is in the actual genre of the writings. The Second Reading is taken from one of the apostolic *letters*. The *gospel* genre arose several decades later in order to meet a growing need in the life of the first communities, the need for a more extended narrative of the life of Jesus. This would keep the concentration on the Death and Resurrection found in the letters from turning into an abstraction. There was much to remember about Jesus' whole life, and numerous stories from it were naturally in circulation. There were his many memorable words and encounters with others, his marvelous parables, the miracles he worked from kindness and compassion, his various practices, most notably his habit of "eating and drinking with sinners" (see Luke 15:2). The four Gospels that were eventually accepted into the canon—again, like the letters, because in them the Church recognized the living faith that was passed on from the apostles—were the products of authors from the apostolic era who gathered particular stories into a certain order and told a whole story emphasizing particular theological points that would have been useful to the communities for which they wrote. The evangelist Luke gives us the clearest glimpse into the work of these inspired authors, and we see here that inspiration does not preclude the work and thought of the human author. He says, "Many have undertaken to compile a narrative of the events which have been fulfilled in our midst, precisely as those events were transmitted to us by the original eyewitnesses and ministers of the word. I too have carefully traced the whole sequence of events from the beginning, and have decided to set it in writing for you . . . " (Luke 1:1–3). There are, as Luke suggests here, many ways of compiling a narrative; and now Luke has chosen his own. But what we find in common with all those who "traced the whole sequence of events from the beginning" is that they all agree on the center and climax of the story. It is always the Death and Resurrection of Jesus. Whatever is told is part of this story and helps us to deepen our grasp of it.

It is worth recalling in the context of the Gospel reading what we have already said in general about the event character of the proclamation of the Word. As we hear the Gospel being read, we should be aware that this is not just that particular deacon or priest standing at the ambo and reading out loud from a big book more or less effectively. The proclamation of the Gospel is a mystery, and through it something is happening now! Jesus himself visits the assembly in a very concrete form, speaking today to us these words, working this miracle, telling this parable, eating and drinking with these sinners. But there is more. Whatever particular Gospel we hear on a given day leads us that way that day toward the center. And so what is ultimately happening is that Jesus visits the assembly as the one who was crucified and is now risen.

The evangelist John reports Jesus referring to his Death and Resurrection as his "hour." His hour is an hour that never passes away, never fades into the past, never grows stale or old with the passage of time. So, his hour is what is happening when the Gospel is read. He is present with his very sacrifice, for the one whose entire life in all its details led inexorably to this Death of which all the Law and Prophets spoke—this one is present now, for he is risen from the dead. When we come in subsequent chapters to discussing the Liturgy of the Eucharist, we will see that the ritual and words of that part of the Mass say and accomplish in their own way what has already been said in the Liturgy of the Word. They intensify the character of the one event that is the center of all: the Death and Resurrection of Jesus.

I am insisting here on the power of the Gospel event to travel, as it were, from the past to our present. What Jesus once said and did becomes present in our midst as the Gospel is read. But we should think through some of the consequences of this. We have already said that every proclamation of the Word in the liturgy is also an irreducibly new moment: the event of Christ becomes the event of this particular community here and now. Christ comes and is received as an actual communication of salvation to the particular assembly that here and now hears this Word. And thus the Word addresses us in the concrete circumstances in which we find ourselves. It says something about our moment in history, the moment in our particular lives. It is a saving word for us, full of power, and new because this particular community hearing this Gospel event in these circumstances has never existed before.

We want to recall here also what we have said about being attentive to the direction in which the liturgy is moving. We can see in the proclamation of the Gospel an intensification and a climax of the movement of God the Father toward the world. To express this in its Trinitarian and ecclesial shape: clearly now what the Father says to the Church is Jesus Christ. When we hear him, when we see him act, we should be mindful that this is the Father's Word given to us. What he says and does reveals the Father. His Death and Resurrection reveals the Father. This Word reaches its mark in the hearts of those who hear it because it comes accompanied by the Holy Spirit, just as Christ first came into the world accompanied by the Spirit. The Spirit ensures that Jesus Christ sinks down, way down, into the community which stands in reverence, awe, and wonder listening to the Gospel. We cry out to the very one who is now present among us: "Praise to you, Lord Jesus Christ!"

The Gospel is always read by a deacon or a priest, or by the bishop himself if there are no other ordained ministers present at the Eucharist where he presides. This is a ritual "rule," which is part of the serious game of the liturgy. It is a way of playing that helps us to understand that the Gospel is the privileged center of the Christian Bible and that its proclamation in the liturgy is the privileged climax of the Liturgy of the Word. It alerts us to the fact that Christ himself is now speaking directly to his assembled Church. Further, the bishop is a successor to the apostles. He ordains deacons to proclaim the Gospel, and this mission remains in those deacons whom he later ordains as priests. Reserving the proclamation of the Gospel to the ordained reminds us that the Gospel expresses apostolic faith in a preeminent way. Since the Gospel is not unrelated to the rest of Sacred Scripture, which has been read by some of the baptized but not ordained members of the community, this rule of the ritual game is an implicit reminder that all of Sacred Scripture is read and understood under the authority of apostolic faith. The bishop and anyone whom he has ordained are meant to represent this apostolic guarantee.

The Homily

For this same reason the homily that now follows is also reserved to one of the ordained. This is not to say that lay people might not be just as insightful about the meaning of Sacred Scripture and just as effective in speaking publicly about them. Indeed, just on the level of insight and speaking, it is obvious that sometimes lay people could be even more effective than the ordained. Though it is certainly desirable that the ordained be insightful and effective preachers, that is not the first point about reserving the preaching of the homily to them. Again, it is an injunction of the ritual that tells both the one preaching and the assembly listening what is to be expected in this moment. This is not the time for mere personal insight or for the spinning out of individual theories and stories. That one of the ordained is preaching is meant to be a guarantee in the assembly that what is heard is the Church's apostolic faith and not merely the private thoughts and experiences of an individual. Of course, that faith is carried in the whole body of believers. But ordination includes the responsibility of representing this faith in a public, verifiable way. The bishop's communion with the other bishops of the world through his communion with the pope is the verifiable assurance that from this bishop we hear the faith of the apostles. And the communion of priests and deacons with their bishop is the same verifiable assurance. The bishop has carefully watched over the training of those whom he ordains as deacons and priests, making certain that they are capable of representing apostolic faith.

If we use our method of attending to what direction the liturgy is moving now in order to understand something of the homily, we will see that in fact the homily is a delicate combination of both directions. It is first of all the direction of responding to what God has said. It is the preacher's responsibility to listen with special care to all that is said in the now of today's liturgy by means of the particular texts that have been proclaimed. On the basis of this careful listening, he will propose to the assembly ways of ensuring that God's word finds its home in our hearts and that we respond to it as we ought. So, if in one sense the word is coming into him, in another sense it is coming out of him. He is in the middle position. Jesus Christ is the Word that comes in, and Jesus Christ is meant to be the Word that comes out.

A great tradition supports the preacher in this delicate task. It is what I have been calling apostolic faith. What the apostles experienced and believed has been handed on, "traditioned" on through the centuries. Jesus entrusted his mission to the apostles, and it has been handed on through their successors, reaching as far as us. This fact, this shape of God's plan, is represented in the preaching of the bishop and those he has ordained. The commission to preach, which the apostles received from the Lord, parallels the Lord's own receiving of his mission from the Father. We have already noted that the risen Lord said to his disciples, "As the Father has sent me, so I send you" (John 20:21). This "as" and "so" express a huge mystery; indeed, nothing less than an echo of the Trinitarian mystery in which the Son comes forth from the Father. In that same way, from those same mysterious depths, the apostolic preacher comes forth from the risen Lord. Thus, the pattern according to which the Lord preached must become the pattern of every Christian preacher. Jesus expressed that pattern precisely: "My teaching is not my own but is from the one who sent me" (John 7:16).

Even so, there is a difference in kind between the preaching of Jesus and the preaching of the apostles. Jesus, though bearing testimony to the Father, also bears testimony to himself (Luke 4:21; John 3:11; 5:31–47; 8:14–18; 10:25; 15:26; 1 Timothy 6:13; 1 John 5:7–8). The apostles for their part bear testimony not to themselves but to Jesus. He indeed becomes the principal content of their preaching. Beginning with the preaching ascribed to Peter in the Acts of the Apostles, the texts of the Old Testament are referred to Jesus, to his Death and Resurrection. This use of the scriptural text in reference to the Lord's Paschal Mystery becomes the basis of all preaching. Explaining the text in this way becomes the preacher's task. The methods of interpretation and the reasoned defense of the new faith as found in the sermons of Peter and Paul in Acts are followed up and developed by the Fathers. To understand why the Fathers preached the way they did, one must realize that they themselves saw what they were doing to be a continuation of the apostolic preaching. What will develop in patristic preaching is based on decisions made in the apostolic preaching. Peter's sermon on Pentecost can summarize the method. To explain the extraordinary things that had just happened, Peter begins by saying, "This is that which was spoken by the prophet Joel" (Acts 2:16. The basic sermons are Acts 2:14–36; 3:12–26; 4:8–12; 5:29–32; 10:34–43; 13:16–41; 14:14–17; 17:22–31. Jesus himself set this pattern in Luke 4:16–22; 24:25–27, 44–47).

That this kind of preaching begins on Pentecost is no accident. If from one angle it can be said that Christian preaching derives from the risen Lord, from a different angle it can be said to be the fruit of Pentecost, the gift of the Spirit. A solid theological principle to employ in seeking to discern what the Spirit is doing in the Church is to remember what Paul himself learned from the Spirit: "No one can say, 'Jesus is Lord,' except by the Holy Spirit" (1 Corinthians 12:3). And further, "God sent the Spirit of his Son into our hearts, crying out, 'Abba, Father!'" (Galatians 4:6). This defines the preacher's task: to enable the whole community and each individual believer to say with one's whole being, "Jesus is Lord," and to cry out "Abba, Father!" to God. This is a task of infinite proportions and inexhaustible wealth. To preach Christ is to preach "the mystery of God," to preach the one "in whom are hidden all the treasures of wisdom and knowledge" (Colossians 2:2–3). This infinite wealth begins to unfold in the Church from the time of the apostles and is developed in the patristic centuries. Preaching in our own times should be marked by continuity with this apostolic and patristic heritage.

The homily during Mass, however, has a task beyond preaching the Sacred Scriptures in this way. It must also signal and to some extent explain the link between the Liturgy of the Word, which is now concluding, and the Liturgy of the Eucharist, which is about to begin. As we shall see in the following chapters, in some mysterious sense the Eucharistic liturgy echoes the pattern of the Word becoming flesh in the mystery of the Incarnation. The scriptural words proclaimed in the liturgy become sacrament; that is, the ritual actions and words performed around the community's gifts of bread and wine proclaim in their own way at an even deeper level the one and only event of salvation: the Lord's Death and Resurrection. And they proclaim that event as the very event of the community's celebration.

Preaching during the Eucharist must speak of these things. The preacher must be capable of explaining them, proclaiming them, lifting the community's minds and hearts up toward them. All the texts must be brought to the event that encompasses them: the Lord's Death and Resurrection. That through the Eucharist about to be celebrated we have communion in the very same Death and Resurrection—this too must be proclaimed and explained.

THE CREED OR PROFESSION OF FAITH

After the homily the Creed or Profession of Faith is said on Sundays and Solemnities. Why is it placed here? The Creed is a summary of the Church's way of reading the Sacred Scriptures, and consequently it is a summary of the Church's faith. It is not something in addition to Sacred Scripture; it is Sacred Scripture reduced to a single page. If the vast and multifaceted text of the Sacred Scriptures are the tens of thousands of pieces of a mosaic, the Creed is the master plan for how the pieces fit together. The Nicene Creed is usually used, but in certain circumstances the Apostles' Creed may be used. This book is not the place for a commentary on the Creed. That would be a huge task. In fact, *The Catechism of the Catholic Church*—no small text—is in effect an expansive commentary. But a few remarks can be helpful here for understanding what is happening when we recite the Creed at Mass.

The Creeds have their origins in the liturgy of Baptism, where, before adults were baptized in the name of the Trinity, they had first to profess faith in the Holy Trinity. This profession of faith had a three-fold structure. The one to be baptized would either answer three questions or profess three statements in which in effect he or she said, "I believe in God the Father, in Jesus Christ his only Son, and in the Holy Spirit." The three parts of this profession were called articles, and each was more or less expanded to state in summary form the essential ingredients of what is believed about the Father, the Son, and the Holy Spirit and their relationship to each other. The second article on Jesus Christ was the most developed.

Belief in the Holy Trinity is not belief in an *idea* about God. It is belief in the *persons* of Father, Son, and Holy Spirit; that is, belief in the divine life revealed to us in the Death and Resurrection of Jesus, as this is preached and known in the Church that comes from the apostles. There is no other way of knowing the Trinitarian mystery than through this community. And so the profession of faith in the Trinity includes also a profession of belief in the Church, as one, holy, catholic, and apostolic. The Church is the context in which the divine life of the Trinity is shared with its members for "the forgiveness of sins . . . / the resurrection of the dead / and the life of the world to come." In speaking of the overall shape of the liturgy, we observed that in naming Father, Son, and Spirit when describing the twofold movement of the Eucharistic liturgy, it was not possible to do so without also naming Church and world. The same is true inside the Creed. We believe not only in God but in what the Church tells us of God and of our life in God.

The Creed is not sung very often anymore, and this is too bad. In fact, throughout history there is ample precedent for both singing and reciting the Creed. But in the ideal liturgy that we are imagining as the basis on which to build our theological reflection, I think it is helpful to imagine the words of the Creed sung by the assembly to a solemn, noble, joyful musical setting. We would hear then our many voices blending together into the one single voice of the Church, and we would feel immediately the beauty of the reality of the Church's clear and precise understanding of all that the Sacred Scriptures say. There are ancient melodies for the Creed that have been sung for centuries. In singing that same song we would feel the thrill of knowing that ours is the same faith as Christians from all the previous generations, expressed with these same words for nearly two thousand years. Such a way of proclaiming the Creed would help us to understand that we are not merely reciting what can at first glance seem to be a rather technical and abstract summary of our faith. Instead, as the Liturgy of the Word comes to its conclusion, the assembly stands and with one voice declares all that the apostolic Church believes in its careful listening to the Word of God.

The baptismal origins of the Creed are important reminders to us that Baptism and the faith into which we were plunged at Baptism are the only doors through which we can enter into the Liturgy of the Eucharist which is about to begin. The Creed is the Church's ultimate response of faith to God's movement toward her. In each particular Eucharistic assembly that recites it, every baptized person confirms again his or her belonging to the community that believes these things. This is the community, larger and older than the sum of the parts gathered, that is about to celebrate the Eucharist. How tremendous is the Amen that resounds at the end of the Creed, echoing round the globe, echoing through the centuries, echoing in the halls of heaven. I think of one musical setting where the "Ah—" of this Amen goes on and on, climbing quickly into high registers, dropping dramatically into the lower ones, covering forward and backward the whole scale. When I sing it, I never want it to end. In fact, it never does.

The Universal Prayer

In the ritual book that contains the texts and ritual instructions for Mass (called the Roman Missal), the clear order of the Eucharistic liturgy is laid out, with a precisely located shift from the Liturgy of the Word to the Liturgy of the Eucharist. The last part of the Liturgy of the Word is what is called the Universal Prayer, the Prayer of the Faithful. But as the last part it is also useful to consider it as a hinge swinging us into the next part.

The bishop or priest presides at this ritual moment, opening it with an introduction and inviting the people to pray. He is a sacrament of Christ at the head of his body. Christ leads his people in prayer. The movement is a movement of the assembly toward God the Father. Christ stands in the middle position. Our coming to the Father is through him. Then a deacon or some other person articulates particular prayers on behalf of the assembly, and the assembly adds its own voice to each one together. It can be effective if these petitions are sung, but sung or not, the series of petitions creates a pulsing rhythm as the Church cries out her needs before the heavenly Father.

These are called the Universal Prayer, as an indication of the direction in which our prayer ought to go. These petitions should be very broad, all-embracing. Individuals can pray for their particular needs in the quiet of their hearts. Here the Church is giving voice to her relationship with the whole world. These intercessions are also called the Prayer of the Faithful (*faithful* being an almost technical word used by tradition to describe the baptized) because it is the responsibility of the baptized persons who live in the world to bring before God in prayer the needs of the Church and the whole world. It is precisely their life in the world, enlightened and shaped by what they have heard today in the Word of God, that equips these people with a knowledge of what to pray for.

In describing the twofold movement of the liturgy, we noted that God addresses Himself to the world not vaguely but through the Church. The Church exists for the sake of the world and speaks a word of response to God in the name of the whole world. So, at this moment in the liturgy the direction is a movement of response to God's word on the part of the Church and for the sake of the world. It is this role of the Church that is articulated now in this prayer. The bishop inviting the faithful to articulate the prayer is the ritual expression—the mystery—of Christ entrusting to his body a responsibility in the world. By his own example Christ has taught us what and whom to care about. Now he waits for us to have a heart and mind like his. This is nothing less than his sharing with us his priestly role of interceding for the world. After we have expressed our needs, he himself will gather them together and make them his own, in the same way that the bishop will conclude the prayer: "through Christ our Lord."

I want to insist on the breadth that these prayers should have. If particular communities do not manage to think in their prayers beyond their own borders and interests, it is a foreshortened sense of Church that is being expressed. In the community that reflects Christ's own expansive heart, we pray first of all for the Church, but for the

Church precisely so that she can be holy and pleasing to God and a sacrament of salvation for the world. And we pray for the world, above all that the world may know the salvation offered in Christ and, short of that, that sufferings and hardships be relieved, that injustices be redressed. We pray mindful of God's intentions for the world; namely, that "all people might be saved and come to knowledge of the truth" (1 Timothy 2:4). Or, put another way, we pray knowing that God intends that all the peoples of the world be gathered around the Eucharistic table where we are now gathered. And so all that we are privileged to pray and say there, all that we shall receive there, we shall do in their name.

In the next part of the liturgy, where the Liturgy of the Eucharist begins, gifts of bread and wine, as well as other gifts, will be collected from the faithful and brought forward in procession to the priest. We will have a good deal to say about all that. But now, considering the Universal Prayer as a hinge, we can say that all that we pray for now will be brought forward with the bread and wine and placed in Christ's hands for transformation. The Church brings both herself and the world forward and petitions transformation.

*   *   *

So the second major part of the Mass is called as a whole the Liturgy of the Eucharist. In turn, there are parts to this part, and they will be treated in the following three chapters. Those parts are the Preparation of the Gifts, the Eucharistic Prayer, and the Communion Rite. Much has happened already, but even more happens now—unimaginably more!

Chapter Four

The Preparation of the Gifts

COLLECTING THE GIFTS

While the people are seated, some from among them begin to collect the gifts. Even if the bread and wine, which will be transformed in the Eucharistic sacrifice, have already been prepared and set out in advance, it is important for us to think of these as likewise collected now. In the same way that an intricate story of grace stands behind the arrival of each member of the assembly into the one place where the Eucharist will be offered, so also many stories—whole lives—are being collected now and represented in bread and wine. We also bring forward money, and we should not think of the collection of money at this point as some sort of banal, dirty but necessary affair. Money is our work. Money is hours of our lives. And now we give it away, we sacrifice it, for the work of the Church, which in the end is its work of charity and evangelization. In the oldest description we have of the Mass from the second century, Saint Justin already speaks of the collection of money at this point in the liturgy.

But more than something merely practical, like the collecting of funds, is happening now. One of the principal words with which the tradition has understood the Mass is to speak of it as a sacrifice. We will need to use this word and pay attention to it again and again to understand all that unfolds in the ritual from this point on. Obviously the Mass is not some sort of primitive sacrifice in which animals are put to death or other gifts immolated to placate God. There is a precise Christian understanding to the term that can only become clear as we watch how it is used throughout what follows. Saint Paul helps us to understand this specific Christian sense. For him the Death and Resurrection of Christ and our communion in these have introduced an entirely new reality into the world, beginning from Christ's submission to the Jewish Law, but extending outward from there to include all Gentiles with a share in the promise. As a result, the Old Law and its sacrifices no longer have validity. There is a new covenant and a new kind of sacrifice. At the end of his impressive and moving meditation on the enigma of Israel's refusal to believe in Jesus Christ in chapters 9 to 11 of the letter to the Romans, Saint Paul starts up a new line of thought in chapter 12 describing the life of Christians in clear distinction from unbelieving Israel. The first sentence of this exhortation reads, "I urge you, *therefore,* by the mercies of God to offer your bodies as a living sacrifice, holy and pleasing to God, your spiritual worship" (Romans 12:1). So the new sacrifice of Christians, as opposed to the animal sacrifices offered in the Temple, is the very body of the Christian offered to God in a holy life. This is called "spiritual worship" as opposed to the carnal worship of animal sacrifices. Our bodies as a living sacrifice—this is what the collection of gifts is meant to enact. But Christians do not offer up their lives by themselves. They can only do it through, and with, and in Christ's offering. This is what is enacted in what follows.

Bringing the Gifts to the Bishop or Priest

The procession with the gifts offers us one of the strongest opportunities for understanding the relation between the sacrifice of the Christian people and the sacrifice of Christ. Gifts of bread and wine are brought to the altar. It is an action worth examining as if under a microscope. A joyful procession accompanied by song (the Offertory Chant) starts down the aisle of the church. Bread and wine and various vessels and water and perhaps other gifts, often including money, are carried by some of the baptized and brought to the bishop and/or deacon who places the bread and wine on the altar and prepares them.

Yet to understand the significance of the bread and wine we must look further and leave the church building to discover where this bread and wine have come from. It is worth tracing them all the way back to their literal, earthly roots—back to wheat planted in a field, its sprouting during a different season, its being cared for by skilled farmers, its coming to maturity and being harvested. Then it is ground and brought to bakers who exert their own skills and bake bread in their ovens. And something similar must occur for the wine. Vines are cared for, pruned and cultivated, and grapes are gathered. There is need for the vintner's skills and the years of the wine coming to maturity in the cellar. Already many people have been involved, and seasons and years have had to pass so that we might have the bread and wine brought forward in today's liturgy. Still others bring these gifts from the baker and the winery, purchasing them with funds earned in some other work. Thus it is that we may call the bread and wine the fruits of creation and history, the fruits of nature combined with human ingenuity: "fruit of the earth and work of human hands." It is of great importance that we notice carefully that these fundamental symbols of the Eucharistic liturgy are not purely natural symbols, as is, say, water in Baptism. They are in fact the product of the cooperation between the Creator and human beings.

It is true that bread and wine have their precise meaning in the context of the Passover and in the Lord's Last Supper and that bread and wine are involved here in obedience to his command to do this in memory of him. But we can reflect as well on the fittingness of the Lord's choice and what the Spirit had prepared. Bread and wine in fact are extremely strong symbols, powerful and rich in what they express. Perhaps nothing summarizes so well the deepest experience of what it means to be a human being and what we most desire.

We are not animals that snatch food from the ground or from trees with our mouths, roaming about alone until our stomachs are full enough to get us through to the next round. We produce our food together, we consume it together, we share it with one another. It is an expression of love and desire. It aims at communion. We can hardly imagine life without this—not because we are gluttons but because we were made this way. Food is both a substance needed to stay alive and a symbol needed to stay human. With food we tell one another that we love one another, that we are dependent on one another, that we desire the other to live and be well. If bread is the most fundamental end of the food spectrum, wine is its festive end. Wine testifies to the technical and aesthetic capacity of human beings. It is a refined and elegant way to say what we say more simply with bread: we love one another, we desire the other to live and be well. In a word, bread and wine aim at communion. They are already a language. Christ will transform them and make them say inconceivably more.

As these gifts are collected from outside the church and brought into the church, finally brought down the aisle to the hands of the bishop, there is articulated in this ritual action not only the relation between the order of the ordained priesthood and the order of the baptized. In seeing this we see articulated also the global relationship between Church and world, between Church and all creation, between Church and all history. Through the work of the baptized in the world, the Church brings to the hands of Christ the fruits of the creation and the work of human hands. This is an exercise of the priesthood of the faithful. These gifts are an offering with which we would wish to give thanks to the Father for all that He has done for us, in creating us and still more wonderfully in redeeming us. But what offering could be made that would be worthy thanks to the Father? In fact, there is nothing. We have brought all we have, and yet we know that it could never be enough to be a suitable, worthy thanksgiving offered to the Father.

Nonetheless, it is precisely in this condition of poverty before God that Christ comes to meet us and reveal his solidarity with us in this poverty. He will take our gifts into his hands, and he will transform them into his very Body and Blood, transform them into his Paschal Sacrifice that he is continually offering in heaven. I am directing our attention to the very stuff, to the material out of which the saving event of Christ's sacrifice is to be made to occur in our midst. God's Word to us is Jesus Christ, and not just vaguely Jesus Christ but Jesus Christ above all in the action of his dying and rising. And this Word will now be articulated to us in the syllables and words and phrases of bread and wine transformed. They become a language. The name of this language is flesh. It is our flesh, our lives, we who brought the gifts. Our gifts become the Word made flesh. Thereby the whole creation and the whole of history are rendered capable of something that, by definition, would be impossible to them. They are rendered capable of being God's adequate expression of himself. More: they are rendered capable of being an offering to God the Father, of being the thanksgiving and adoration that Christ's very sacrifice on the cross was and is.

So, it is not a throwaway phrase to say that we offer up our lives to God. This is a phrase full of meaning; indeed, we could say it summarizes the whole economy of salvation. But, as we have said, Christians do not offer up their lives by themselves. They can only do it through, and with, and in Christ's offering. In the course of the rite when bread and wine are brought to the hands of the bishop by some of the baptized, a magnificent exchange begins to take shape. We bring our lives—with all our efforts to produce and to be together in love, with all our desire and our willingness to share—and we place them in the hands of Christ by placing them in the hands of the bishop. (The bishop or priest is in this moment the sacrament of Christ the head, who leads his whole body in offering his sacrifice.) Implicitly, something is said by this action that will be explicitly articulated later in the Eucharistic

Prayer. Basically the action is our saying to Christ, "Do something with this. Make our lives be what your life was and is."

THE PRAYERS OF PRESENTATION

After the procession the altar is prepared, and the bread and wine are set out on it. The priest comes to the altar, picks up the bread, and says a short prayer. In this action we see Christ begin his action of leading our prayer. Into his hands we have placed our gifts; from his hands they will be offered to the Father. If the community is still singing, the priest says the prayer inaudibly. Otherwise, he may say it aloud, and the people respond with a short acclamation. The prayer, audible or not on any given day, says explicitly in just a few words what the collection and the procession have said implicitly and more extensively. God is blessed for the gift of bread, explicitly acknowledged, as we have said, as something that is "fruit of the earth and work of human hands." Something similar is prayed over the wine. The transformation of both is anticipated, and we feel the pull of what is about to happen. "[I]t will become for us the bread of life . . . / it will become our spiritual drink."

LITTLE MYSTERIES

Three other little moments of the ritual are worth noticing at this point. They are very ancient actions, and they express so much when we understand their meaning. I call them little mysteries because even if they do not constitute the essential action of this part of the rite, they nonetheless are concrete somethings through which the transcendent dimension of what is happening shines through.

Water Mixed with Wine

The first of these mysteries is the deacon or priest pouring wine into the chalice and then mixing a little water into the wine as he does so. The words he says inaudibly call this action a mystery. He says, "By the mystery of this water and wine / may we come to share in the divinity of Christ, / who humbled himself to share in our humanity." On the purely natural level, diluting wine with water was common in the ancient world and so simply a part of preparing the wine. But in this concrete something, somebody early on noticed in this a wonderful image for understanding our communion with the sacrifice of Christ. Of the two elements, wine and water, wine is the more precious, and so let it represent divinity. The water placed in the wine represents our poor humanity, which will be completely joined to Christ's divinity in the course of what follows. As early as the middle of the third century Saint Cyprian of Carthage was talking this way. He said that we should never offer the wine without water since that would be like offering Christ without his people. It is a little gesture, a bonus, if you will, but it has long been done and is a striking mystery.

Incense

The relation between the gifts that the people bring and their very bodies and lives is manifested with special clarity in the liturgy when incense is used at this point. First, the gifts themselves are incensed, which is a ritual gesture (serious play) marking them out as holy. It is as if we can feel the immediate future already invading these gifts. Bread and wine that soon will become his Body and Blood are already somehow holy! Then the altar is marked out as holy. The table on which the gifts lie is designated as the holy place that is truly the center of the world: the place of Christ's Paschal Sacrifice. Then the incensing action shifts to honor the bishop as head of the body, after which the whole body, the assembly, is incensed to indicate that they themselves are what lies on the altar. The whole church becomes a sweet smelling offering rising up to the Father; the whole church becomes a mysterious and holy place precisely because of what is about to happen. I say "the whole church," meaning first of all a building; but the building and the assembly that fills it are now manifesting a mystery, such that we may say that the whole Church everywhere in the world is this sweet smelling offering, and that mystery is manifested now in this particular assembly.

Washing the Hands

Next the priest stands at the side of the altar and washes his hands, saying inaudibly a verse from a psalm: "Wash me, O Lord, from my iniquity / and cleanse me from my sin." Again, on a purely natural level there once would have been need for this washing. The handling of many gifts could possibly have been messy, and even today after handling the incense and swinging the thurible, washing serves a practical need. The line from the psalm is a bonus accompanying this practical gesture and a reminder to the priest that the level of action is about to shift. As the people see him washing his hands, they too should be reminded of the same. Our gifts have been brought forward and arranged on the altar. The hands of the priest turn now to a new purpose. Now Christ will make the hands of the priest his own hands, for there is only one priest, and the hands that will take up these gifts, transform them, and offer them to the Father, are the hands of Christ.

The Prayer over the Offerings

We have brought our lives in sacrifice to be joined to the sacrifice of Christ, and so the priest urges, "Pray, brothers and sisters / that my sacrifice and yours / may be acceptable to God, / the almighty Father." The people rise to their feet and respond with a short prayer that refers to the priest's hands, naming what is about to happen as "the sacrifice at your hands." Our sacrifice is offered only through Christ. The final prayer is called the Prayer over the Offerings. This varies from Sunday to Sunday, from feast to feast; but it always mentions in some form the gifts we have brought and prays for their transformation and ours. When we say Amen to this prayer, we are saying Amen to all that has happened from the collecting of the gifts to this moment. Now we stand poised for the biggest prayer of all.

Chapter Five

The Eucharistic Prayer

The Eucharistic Prayer begins with the Preface dialogue (where the priest says, "The Lord be with you," then "Lift up your hearts," then "Let us give thanks . . . ") and extends through to the great Amen. What happens during this prayer is stunning. The mind reels before the mystery. The heart is thrilled. Belief strains. And yet in every generation people keep coming back again and again to hold themselves before the unbelievable experience of this prayer, hoping each time to penetrate its mystery more deeply, to participate in it more entirely, to perceive what happens during the prayer and to be a part of it. It is the biggest prayer the Church has. She exists to pray it, and she comes into being by praying it.

There are a number of different parts to the prayer, and here more than ever our method of following closely the ritual shape and texts will serve to help us understand better all that is happening. We will go through the parts one by one, seeing how an enormous momentum builds throughout, climaxing in the whole creation joined to the whole of heaven in a perfect act of praise directed to God the Father, through Jesus Christ, in the Holy Spirit.

Before going through each of the parts, it will be useful to pull together in this context some key concepts we have already used to understand other parts of the Mass. First of all, in the Eucharistic Prayer, all that we have said about the event character of the proclamation of the Word reaches a new intensity. One of the major strands that runs through the Eucharistic Prayer is what could be called a narrative strand. In a way similar to what we already saw with the Sacred Scriptures, where the words recall all the great events of our salvation, the text of the Eucharistic Prayer recalls great events. But now the narration is entirely concentrated on the center. We remember the Death and Resurrection of Jesus Christ. Here when we say, "remember events" we mean far more than a thin monotone of words pronounced aloud. We mean a narrative in which words are surrounded by gestures and signs and indeed an entire elaborate meal in a particular place and with particular people. In this elaborate act of remembering, still in virtue of Jesus' Resurrection, that original event becomes the event of the community that hears it. From Sunday to Sunday and from feast to feast, the readings from Sacred Scripture change in order to lay out portions of the whole story through the course of the year. But in every Mass, no matter what the feast, during the Eucharistic Prayer the same story, the one and only center, is proclaimed. On Christmas Day, when in Sacred Scripture we remember the events surrounding Jesus' birth, at the climax of our gathering we still tell the central story of his Death and Resurrection, and that telling is the climax of the Christmas feast.

To understand what happens during the Eucharistic Prayer we will also want to pay more attention than ever to the directions of the twofold movement that we have already observed in other parts of the liturgy. After the opening dialogue before the Preface, where the bishop and assembly speak back and forth to one another in three short and intense exchanges, the words of this prayer are addressed entirely to God the Father. In this sense, then, the direction of movement is clearly from the Church toward the Father. As always, the Church speaks not only in her own name but also intends to represent the whole world, indeed, the whole creation. The Trinitarian shape of the movement is also clearly present. The entire prayer is directed to the Father, through the Son, in the Holy Spirit.

Yet, there is likewise a very clear movement in the prayer from the Father toward the Church; for in fact, the Church pleads in this prayer for the Father to send the Holy Spirit on the gifts of bread and wine, and the Father does so. We ask for this so that our gifts might be transformed into the Body and Blood of His Son, and this entreaty is answered. And so in the prayer the Father comes toward the Church by sending His Son, accompanied by the Holy Spirit. To follow with attention the twofold direction of movement can be staggering, but that is our task, and it is the joy of our prayer. We ask the Father to send His Son and Spirit. They come and do something! Something happens! They transform the bread and wine that we have brought into the Body and Blood of the Son, and concomitant with that they make us one body, one spirit in that Body of the Son. Then through the Son and in the Spirit the Church offers this Body to the Father! We will trace this tremendous, swirling movement and its directions throughout the various parts of the prayer.

Another thought might be useful in helping us hold together as a whole all the various parts of the prayer we are about to examine. When I talk with my students about this prayer, I express to them an admittedly impossible desire. First I tell them of the importance of holding all the dimensions and directions of the prayer in dynamic relationship with each other. Something similar is required for the various roles of Father, Son, and Holy Spirit and what each does through-out the course of the prayer. Then I express my impossible desire: to be able to have emerge from my mouth two, three, and four discourses at once, in such a way that we would not think that there comes first, for example, what the Son does with all that this may mean and then, after this, what the Spirit does with all that this may mean. Or vice versa. Or that first there is the movement toward the Father, and then only after this his movement toward us. Or vice versa. But since my desire is an impossible one, it is necessary to proceed step by step. I talk about one thing after another, and I must do the same here. Still, what the mouth cannot do, the mind can. That is, after all has been said—or in the present case, written—then the mind must conceive of all the dimensions as occurring at once, as simultaneously unfolding and reacting to each other, as variously overlapping, as tones and counter tones that make sense only in relation to what they sound against.

The words and gestures of this prayer are mysteries. So, as concrete somethings they can only be said and done one after another. But in the divine reality to which they refer and with which they put us in contact, there is not a one after another but only an all at once. We enter into the hour of Christ. We enter into the all at once of his Resurrection, where the past he once lived is still present to him and made available to us as the event we are undergoing. But we likewise enter into a future that he has already achieved and established where all things in heaven and on earth are recapitulated in him, where we are already standing forever with the angels and saints in heaven. And we do not encounter first Christ, and then the Spirit, and then the Father—or some variation on this order. There is no encounter and no action that is not the three in one simultaneously. This is the divine reality. We are spliced into it concretely in one ritual gesture and word after another—spliced in through these mysteries.

We turn now and follow the prayer through its various parts.

THE PRIEST SPEAKS FIRST TO THE PEOPLE— THE PREFACE DIALOGUE

After the Prayer over the Offerings and the people's Amen, which concludes the Preparation of the Gifts, all the energy of our prayer shifts onto a new level. This shift is signaled by the priest summoning the assembly onto the new level in three short and intense exchanges with them. These ritual verses are very ancient. We have evidence for their being used at this point in the Eucharistic liturgy in texts as old as the late second century.

In the first of these exchanges the priest opens his arms wide and says, "The Lord be with you." The people answer, "And with your spirit." We already saw an exchange like this at the very beginning of the liturgy. What would be the reason for repeating such a greeting now in the middle? After all, priest and people have had plenty of exchange already up to this point. The greeting is repeated precisely because we are going to start praying now with much greater intensity, and if we are to manage it, we will need divine help. The priest wishes the people this divine assistance. His greeting is like a blessing in which he reminds the people that together with him they are about to offer the Church's greatest prayer.

If the assembly needs divine help for its role in what is about to happen, they are aware that even more will be needed by the priest himself, who will play a central and unique role in this prayer. Even greater intensity of attention is required of him as he performs gestures, handles the gifts, and pronounces words the power of which it is impossible entirely to grasp. As we said of this response at the beginning of the Mass, when they say, "And with your spirit," the people are addressing the "spirit" of the priest; that is, that deepest interior part of his being where he has been ordained precisely to lead the people in this sacred action. They are saying in effect, "Be the priest for us now," aware that there is only one priest, Christ himself, and that this one who represents him now must be finely tuned to perform his sacred duties well. If the priest's greeting is like a blessing on the people, the people bless their priest in return. The people know that if their priest is "in this prayer" with all his heart, all his mind, all his soul, this will be to their advantage also; for at every point in the prayer he is their leader, and they cannot advance in it without him.

The priest's leading role throughout the entire Eucharistic Prayer is meant to render concrete for the assembly a fundamental reality of all prayer but especially of this the most intense of prayers. That reality is that the Church addresses itself to the Father only through Christ its head. The priest is a sacrament of Christ signifying this reality. The whole structure of the prayer—with the priest speaking and acting and the people following and saying their Amen at the end—is a concrete something, a mystery, in which we experience Christ as head of the body leading his whole body before the Father. So, in this first of three exchanges, priest and people have acknowledged and lovingly awakened each other to the roles they must play in what follows.

With the next exchange the priest is already and entirely within his role as Christ at the head of his body. With a voice of authority, but a voice also filled with excitement and love for what is about to happen, he commands the people, "Lift up your hearts." In the Latin—*sursum corda*—this phrase is like a shout, literally, "Hearts on high!" It is Christ the head telling his body where we are going, and we're going there fast, so wake up and get on with it. We are going right up into heaven where Christ is seated at the right hand of the Father. All that is about to happen, happens there.

In response to this, the body answers its head and says, "We lift them up to the Lord"; that is, we have our hearts where you told us to put them. We know why you summon us upward, and it is exactly where we want to be with you. In effect, this summons on high is a being brought into the all-at-once of Christ's Resurrection, into his hour, where past and future are both made present to us, where we can already be where we are meant to be for all eternity. Having our hearts on high releases us from our anxieties and daily cares precisely so that we can gain the perspective that allows us to see the ultimate meaning of even these. We are obeying the apostle's injunction when he said, "Since you have been raised up in company with Christ, set your heart on what pertains to higher realms where Christ is seated at God's right hand. Be intent on things above rather than on things of earth. After all, you have died! Your life is hidden now with Christ in God. When Christ our life appears, then you shall appear with him in glory" (Colossians 3:1–3).

In the phrase "your life is hidden now with Christ in God," we should recognize once again the particular Christian sense of the word *mystery* as we have been using it. It always carries a sense of something hidden but also now revealed to the eyes of faith. When we place our hearts on high, we see that the concrete something of our lives is hidden with Christ in God. That is, we are already in heaven where Christ is seated at God's right hand. In the course of this liturgy, "Christ our life appears" in the sacramental forms, and we shall see that we "appear with him in glory." In short, what happens at Mass is that we act out in sacramental form the final and definitive manifestation of Christ, which will include all the members of his body, now hidden in him. That future is already present to those who place their hearts on high in obedience to Christ's invitation.

No sooner are we there in the heavenly place where Christ has taken us, than he announces the purpose of our being there: "Let us give thanks to the Lord our God." The assembly immediately assents to the proposal: "It is right and just." In one immediate sense, within the dynamic of this three-pronged dialogue, what we have to give thanks for is that our hearts are now on high; for this is possible only thanks to the grace of God. But, in fact, our hearts are on high in this hour of Christ as the culmination of all the mighty deeds that God has ever worked for our salvation. And, as we have said many times now, these mighty deeds have a center: the Death and Resurrection of Christ. So it is this for which we shall now gives thanks. Christ himself thanks his Father for his Resurrection, a thanksgiving which includes his joy that we can be made members of his risen body. And for this wondrous gift we, of course, also thank the Father together with him. It is right and just. Nothing could be more right, more just. All that follows is a thanksgiving prayer. Thanksgiving is what the Greek word *Eucharist* means. It is why we can call all that happens at Mass the Eucharist, the thanksgiving.

THE PRIEST BEGINS TO SPEAK TO GOD—THE PREFACE

As soon as the assembly assents to what its leader proposes, the leader turns from the assembly and directs all his attention to the One to whom the thanksgiving prayer is addressed. From now until the end of the prayer, every word is addressed to God the Father and every gesture is performed in His presence. The people follow their leader in his every word and gesture, aware, as the dialogue has expressed, that all of us together, priest and people, must keep our minds and hearts on high—tensed, strained, stretched—through to the end of this prayer, where the people, in the name of the whole creation, will sing their huge Amen to all that their head has accomplished. The voice of the priest is the voice of the assembly, and the assembly has voice only in its priest, and there is only one priest: Jesus Christ.

The prayer that the priest now addresses to God the Father with outstretched arms is called the Preface. We should not be misled by this name. It is the name for this part of the prayer from ancient times not because it is considered a kind of preamble or introduction to the main thing, as the word *preface* connotes in current usage. Its literal Latin sense expresses its meaning here. *Prae-fari* means "to do in front of" or "proclaim in the presence of." So the Preface begins what the entire Eucharistic Prayer will be: a proclaiming and a performing before God the Father of the Church's prayer. It is a prayer that varies from Sunday to Sunday, from feast to feast, and from season to season; but it has a structure that is always the same and always serves the same purpose. Our awareness of this structure will help us to understand what happens when it is prayed. There are three parts. The first part picks up the very words of the last phrase of the preceding dialogue and begins speaking to the Father with the words, "It is truly right and just, our duty and our salvation, / always and everywhere to give you thanks, / Lord, holy Father, almighty and eternal God." The Father is named, variously in different prefaces, with several other of His titles known to us from scripture: Lord, almighty and eternal God.

We want to be sure to notice that the Father is directly addressed: "you . . . / Father." This shows the direction of our prayer in this moment; it is from the Church to God the Father. In this same first part of the preface the phrase that says it is right to give praise *to* the Father often, though not always, states that it is done "*through* Christ our Lord." (If this phrase is not added immediately here, it will appear in the second part of the Preface.) The Trinitarian shape of this movement of direction immediately begins to unfold.

The second part of the Preface always picks up on the phrase "through Christ our Lord" (or inserts it for the first time) and develops it in a way that is unique to each Preface. This is always some succinct expression of what Christ has done for us, phrased to express the particularity of the feast or season. This shape of the prayer, expounded in many different ways but always remembering Christ, can tell us something of the unique way in which Christians give thanks. Giving thanks to the Father consists of far more than simply our good manners, something along the lines of our knowing enough to say thanks to anyone who may have done us a service or a kindness. The biblical way of giving thanks consists in a profound recognition of what God has actually done in what we are thanking Him for. This recognition is expressed by a recounting of what God has done. The biblical word *confess* is a word that often accompanies the thanksgiving of the Church, and it is a word that swings in two directions at once. Recounting what God has done is called "confessing God," and includes praise of Him, both implicitly and explicitly. The greatness of God in His deeds also brings in its wake an awareness of our own smallness and, worse, our infidelity. And so in the same breath we confess our sins. These are not different moments of prayer but various facets of the one action of giving thanks.

We can note also in this second part of the Preface a dimension of prayer that we will want to keep our eye on throughout the whole Eucharistic Prayer; namely, what we can call the narrative strand. We have already mentioned this. Here we want to take note of it for a first time in the Eucharistic Prayer. We are telling again, we are proclaiming aloud, we are confessing the events of God. This is our way of giving thanks.

The third part of the Preface connects with the preceding by always saying (sometimes only implicitly), "And so," or "Therefore . . . ." With this it presents our desire and our request of God that our voices might blend now with the voices of all the angels and saints in singing God's praises. We want to sing because of what we have just remembered in the previous part. This explains the "therefore." We want to sing with the angels and saints because we are conscious of our hearts being on high. We know we are where they are, and we are going to act like it by singing their song. Theirs is a song of continual praise, as many of the Prefaces explicitly state. From our daily cares and anxieties, with our hearts lifted up to where angels and saints are, we share in their continual praise. When this liturgy is over and we must return to life "here below," there will be a sense in which we remain in heaven by means of this song we have joined, a hymn that never ceases.

We have said that the priest's leading this prayer images for the assembly the reality of Christ as head of his praying body. The phrase "through Christ our Lord" in the Preface, as well as the second part which expresses his action on our behalf, give occasion to add a refinement to how we understand this. This will not be the only time that the priest mentions Christ in the course of this prayer. Thus, while it is true that the priest is a sacrament of Christ in his role as head, we are not to imagine somehow that he is Christ. He is an image of Christ but is at the same time distinguishable from him. His is the voice of the assembly, the voice of the Church, speaking through Christ. If we were meant to imagine something as simple as the priest being Christ and everything he says being Christ talking, then it would make no sense in what he says to speak of "Jesus Christ." (Later we will see that during the narrative of the Lord's Supper, the priest will pronounce

Christ's very words over the bread and wine, and in that moment he is a very sharp image of Christ. But he still is not Christ; Christ acts through him. What the priest does, as voice of the Church, he does through Christ. But more on that in its place.)

The *Sanctus* (Holy, Holy, Holy)

The very words of the hymn we sing—"Holy, Holy, Holy . . . "—are revealed to us as a heavenly hymn by several key scriptural texts, which we are certainly meant to recall as we sing these words. These texts unveil for us to some extent the invisible realities into which we are now caught up. There is first of all the vision of God that the prophet Isaiah had when he was caught up in prayer and, as he says, "I saw the Lord seated on a high and lofty throne, with the train of his garment filling the temple." What does the prophet see around the Lord's throne? He describes it: "Seraphim were stationed above; each of them had six wings: with two they veiled their faces, with two they veiled their feet, and with two they hovered aloft." Then he hears them crying aloud one to the other: "Holy, Holy, Holy is the Lord of hosts! All the earth is filled with his glory!" The song was noisy and powerful. He says, "At the sound of that cry, the frame of the door shook and the house was filled with smoke" (Isaiah 6:1–4). It seems that the prophet Ezekiel found himself caught up in the same scene. He says, "Then spirit lifted me up, and I heard behind me the noise of a loud rumbling as the glory of the Lord rose from its place: the noise made by the wings of the living creatures striking one another, and by the wheels alongside them, a loud rumbling" (Ezekiel 3:12–13). In short, we could say that their hearts were on high, where Christ has led our own.

We have said that to the Christian ear all the Old Testament texts and scenes can only be heard to speak of Christ. This is true of the words of the seraphim's song. This is exactly described for us in the book of Revelation, where the apostle John is "caught up in ecstasy on the Lord's day" and "writes on a scroll" the visions he sees of the heavenly liturgy (Revelation 1:10–11). At one point in his vision he sees the very throne of God, surrounded by the same winged creatures that Isaiah and Ezekiel had seen. He too gives us the words of their ceaseless hymn. He tells us, "Day and night, without pause, they sang: 'Holy, Holy, Holy, is the Lord God Almighty, who was, and who is, and who is to come!'" (Revelation 4:8). John's heart, too, is on high, where Christ has led our own.

These visions of the holy prophets and apostle help us to take the measure of all that is happening at Mass when we sing the same words of the angelic song. The singing itself teaches us that we are standing before the very throne of God in heaven. In his visions of the throne of God in heaven, the apostle John always espies as well "the Lamb." We could say that this is a liturgical name for Christ crucified, and John calls what he sees "the throne of God and of the Lamb" (Revelation 22:4). This is astounding! For it means nothing less than that the earthly event of the cross is made a permanent piece of heaven. Or put in the other direction: the cross is a vision on earth of the throne of God. The rest of the words of the hymn we sing plunges our memories immediately into the events of the earthly Cross. We sing, "Hosanna in the highest. / Blessed is he who comes in the name of the Lord. / Hosanna in the highest." Although these are the words of a psalm (Psalm 118:26), they too speak to us of Christ, for they were sung by the people in the very moment when he triumphantly entered Jerusalem, riding on the colt of an ass toward his Passion (Matthew 21:9; Mark 11:10; Luke 19:38). In the rest of the Eucharistic Prayer as it unfolds, we are all the while before the throne of God in heaven; and before the throne of God the sacrifice of the Lamb is all the while present, the hour which does not pass away. Before the throne we sing, "Holy, Holy, Holy." Remembering his entry into Jerusalem to enact his hour we sing, "Blessed is he who comes in the name of the Lord," for we are now standing within that same hour, and we are standing in that hour because he is coming to us now. Blessed is he who comes!

CONFESSING GOD'S HOLINESS AND GLORY

After the assembly sings this hymn, all the people kneel, while the priest alone remains standing and, with outstretched arms, again takes up the prayer directly addressed to God the Father. The people kneeling and the priest alone standing and saying the prayer is meant to indicate even more clearly that the whole body directs its prayer to the Father only through its head, Christ. Kneeling here is meant also as a gesture of adoration. We know now that we are mysteriously raised to heaven itself and that into our very midst there is one "com[ing] in the name of the Lord." That is, Christ is coming; the bread and wine will be changed into his Body and Blood.

Kneeling is the posture at this point in the liturgy in the United States. It is sanctioned by centuries of practice. Other countries assume a posture just as ancient, if not more so: the people remain standing. Both practices are worthy, and each expresses a truth about what is happening that we do well to recall here. If kneeling expresses adoration and reminds us of the holiness of "the hour," standing reminds the assembly that it is active in the prayer even if the priest alone is speaking the words. The members of Christ's body stand with their head and come into the presence of the Father. We have homilies from the fourth and fifth centuries where bishops taught their people that Christians stand for prayer as a sign that we are risen with Christ and pray in the heavenly courts with him.

Whether we kneel or stand during this prayer, it is very important that the assembly be aware that it is actively participating in it. Participation does not happen only when it comes time for me to say something or do something. Listening to and following the prayer is also participation. Standing now or kneeling now is also participation.

We participate in what Christ is accomplishing on our behalf. We go to the Father through Him. All our attention is required for this participation. We must keep our hearts on high—tensed, strained, stretched. We are already mindful of and reaching toward the great Amen, which we will all sing together to close this great prayer.

In the Roman rite since the time of the reform of the liturgy mandated by the Second Vatican Council, one of four different Eucharistic Prayers is chosen for any given celebration of Mass. (Actually there are even more than this, as in Masses for Reconciliation. In other countries Eucharistic Prayers particular to that country have been approved for use. We will not take these into account in our reflections here. The four principal prayers will suffice.) Each of these four prayers has a unique way of unfolding the Eucharistic mystery, and each would merit an extended commentary. That will not be the project here. I will talk in a general way about the elements that are found in all the prayers, even if in each these are differently expressed and developed.

All the prayers begin, as we have already seen, with the dialogue, a Preface, and the singing of the angelic song. Now as the priest continues, he "confesses" God. That is, he speaks to Him with words that acknowledge His glory. The language used is poetic and noble. In acknowledging God we recall before Him the wonders of creation and the great deeds He worked in history for our salvation. We saw this pattern of creation and history already in the Liturgy of the Word. Through both God has spoken to us; through both He has given His Son to the world. Now our words recognize this and celebrate it. "To you, therefore, most merciful Father, / we make humble prayer and petition." Or, "You are indeed Holy, O Lord, / and all you have created / rightly gives you praise." Or, "We give you praise, Father most holy, / for you are great / and you have fashioned all your works / in wisdom and in love."

Poetic language manages to express a lot with a little. The language here is dense, evocative. A single phrase, word, or concept will represent before God whole epochs of what He has done for us. Inevitably the story comes quickly to unfolding its Trinitarian shape. If we acknowledge to the Father what He has done for us, we will come quickly to the Son and the Spirit He has sent to us. "And you so loved the world, Father most holy, / that in the fullness of time / you sent your Only Begotten Son to be our Savior." Or, "for through your Son our Lord Jesus Christ, / by the power and working of the Holy Spirit, / you give life to all things and make them holy." Of course, God already knows these things. He knows what He has done for us. He does not need to learn of them from us. But He wants to hear from us that we know, and this is exactly what we want to say to Him. This is the biblical sense of confessing. We remember before God what He has done, and our narration re-activates in our midst the saving event recalled.

The dense poetic summary at this point in the third Eucharistic Prayer expresses the climax of God's plan for the world as being "so that from the rising of the sun to its setting / a pure sacrifice may be offered to your name." This expression echoes Malachi 1:11, a phrase which the very first generations of Christians saw as a prophecy of the Eucharist. "From the rising of the sun, even to its setting, my name is great among the nations; and everywhere they bring sacrifice to my name and a pure offering." The Christian people were "the nations" of this text, and the Eucharist was their "sacrifice" and "pure offering." The plan of God is to equip us for offering a pure sacrifice to the glory of His name.

Understanding the word *sacrifice* is essential for understanding what is happening now, and we will take note of its occurrences (and related words) throughout all four of the prayers. We are preparing now to offer a sacrifice. We have already recalled the words of Saint Paul to indicate the particular understanding of *sacrifice* that we as Christians have: "I urge you, therefore, by the mercies of God to offer your bodies as a living sacrifice, holy and pleasing to God, your spiritual worship" (Romans 12:1). So the new sacrifice of Christians, as opposed to the animal sacrifices offered in the Temple, is the very body of the Christian offered to God in a holy life. This is called "spiritual worship" as opposed to the carnal worship of animal sacrifices. Our bodies are a living sacrifice, but Christians do not offer up their lives by themselves. They can only do it through, and with, and in Christ's offering. We acknowledge this: "And that we might live no longer for ourselves / but for him who died and rose again for us, / he [Christ] sent the Holy Spirit from you, Father." Or, "To you, therefore, most merciful Father, / we make humble prayer and petition / through Jesus Christ, your Son, our Lord: / that you accept / and bless these gifts, these offerings, / these holy and unblemished sacrifices;" that is, the bread and wine we have brought as the sign of our whole lives.

THE PRIEST CALLS DOWN THE SPIRIT—
THE FIRST EPICLESIS

Epiclesis is a technical liturgical term referring in a strict sense to the invocation to the Father that He send the Holy Spirit on the Church's gifts. More broadly the term can refer to any petitioning of God. Literally in Greek it means "calling down upon." It is a useful word for us to learn and use for understanding what happens at Mass.

We saw that the first movement of prayer after the *Sanctus* (*Holy, Holy, Holy*) was an acknowledgment of what God has done for us in creation and history and an unfolding of the Trinitarian mystery. (In the first and second Eucharistic Prayers this dimension is expressed primarily through the Preface.) Likewise, there is mention of sacrifice as a summary expression for all that God has prepared for us and for what we are about to do. After this first movement of the prayer, there is a notable shift marked by a strong plea. This plea is called the epiclesis. The third Eucharistic Prayer expresses our realization of how much we are about to ask for. It begins, "Therefore, O Lord, we humbly implore you." But we want to catch the logic of the "therefore" in this phrase, which is found in an equivalent position in the other prayers. What we are about to ask for in this moment is based on what God has shown His plan to be; namely, that a perfect offering be made to Him. *Therefore,* we now ask that the bread and wine on the altar become the Body and Blood of Christ. This is the petition of the first epiclesis, "so that they may become for us / the Body and Blood / of our Lord Jesus Christ."

We must remember precisely now that this bread and wine are not just static elements lying there who-knows-why, and they will become who-knows-how the Body and Blood of Christ. This is the bread and wine that we brought, and we say it again in the prayer "these gifts we have brought to you for consecration." And we dare to ask that these be changed into the Body and Blood of Christ because of God's own plan—it's His idea!—that a pure sacrifice may be offered to His name. This prayer is accompanied by a simple but powerful gesture. The priest's hands are stretched out over our bread and wine. It is a rendering visible, if you will, of what is, of course, invisible: the coming of the Spirit into the bread and wine and his causing them to become the Body and Blood of Christ.

The action of the Holy Spirit here in our liturgy exactly parallels the work of the Holy Spirit in the Incarnation of Christ and the work of the Holy Spirit throughout the entire life of Jesus. We (!) experience concretely the unveiling of the Trinitarian mystery in our very midst— concretely because the *Spirit* sent from the *Father* now works to transform our gifts into the Body and Blood of the *Son.* We had pointed ahead to this moment in chapter one when we spoke about the Trinitarian form in the overarching shape of the entire rite. It bears repeating: the Spirit who molded a Body for the Word in the womb of the Virgin Mary, the Spirit who raised the Body of Jesus from the dead—this same Spirit now fills the gifts that the Church brings for transformation and makes them to be one same thing: the Body formed from Mary's body, the Body raised from the dead, Christ's Body made present in the gifts the Church has brought.

It is worth concentrating for a moment on the Spirit's role in the supper the night before Jesus died, for it is especially there that the action of the Holy Spirit in our liturgy exactly parallels the Spirit's role in the life of Jesus. When Jesus took bread and wine into his hands the night before he died, the moment and its possibilities had been long in preparation by the work of the Holy Spirit, "who has spoken through the prophets," as we say in the Creed. That is, the whole of Israel's history had been formed in such a way that it could all converge in this moment and its meaning. The Exodus, around which the entire history centers both before and after, was accomplished fact. Words of the Spirit-formed Scriptures bore testimony to it. A memorial feast given by the Lord brought each new generation of Israelites under its force. Jesus himself had celebrated the feast many times during the course of his life, as had his disciples. A history, a language, a vocabulary, a set of rituals were all in place for Jesus' use in that moment. He takes into his hands what the Spirit had prepared for him; and over it all he pronounces the words that the Spirit with whom he is anointed moves him to utter, "This is my Body, this is my Blood." Thus, together with the Spirit, does he express his own understanding of his mission, which brings the history of Israel to fulfillment. Thus, together with the Spirit, does he express his own willingness to pour out his life for the sake of the many. What the meal shows so magnificently and in so many layered ways—echoing with words and gestures and food, thousands of years of history, and the very creation of the cosmos—the same will be shown in the events that begin to unfold at the end of this very meal: Jesus' arrest, his Death, his Resurrection, his Ascension, the Pentecost of the Spirit. All this the Spirit shapes into the events that are the perfectly articulated Word of the Father to sinful humanity, the life-giving Word of the Father.

But I am getting ahead of myself; my words are outrunning me! I am giving evidence of my impossible desire to have two and three discourses emerge from my mouth at the same time. Let us turn now from the epiclesis, where we see the Spirit's role so clearly, and come to what follows in the prayer, the institution narrative.

The Institution Narrative and Consecration

Now the narrative strand of what the priest is saying comes very much to the fore. A precise and specific event from the life of Jesus is retold; namely, the supper with his disciples the night before he died. It is not the whole supper that is recounted but two specific moments in the course of it, one involving bread and the other involving wine. The priest recounts this story not merely with words but with gestures as well. There is bread and wine present before him, which he uses also to tell the story. There is much that we can reflect on in this part of the prayer, much indeed that happens. Let us first carefully describe the ritual action and words and then attempt to ponder some of what they mean.

We should first of all note the direction of the priest's language. He is still addressing himself to God the Father. This is important. The priest is not doing something so much for the people to hear and see but more so that the Father may hear and see. He performs his narrative before God at an altar in heaven. The people join the priest in this intention. As we have already noted, it is not that God needs to learn of these things from us. It is that when we remember them before Him, He then sees that we know how much He has done for us in His Son. This is the main thing we wish to say to Him: that we know how awesome is the moment we are recalling in His presence.

The priest retells the moment, acting out before the Father in simple stylized gestures what Jesus did and said at the supper. When he tells that Jesus took bread, he picks up the bread that the people have brought in the procession that day. When he tells how Jesus raised his eyes to heaven, he raises his eyes. He relates that Jesus then "said the blessing, / broke the bread, / and gave it to his disciples, saying . . . ." At the point in his telling when the priest comes to what Jesus said, he bows slightly and quotes the very words of Jesus. It is important to note the effect this has. Up to this point the priest tells the story in the past tense, for indeed, what is being remembered before God is a past event. Thus, Jesus *took, blessed, broke, gave, said*—all past tense. It would theoretically be possible to continue in this vein and say, " . . . *said* that the bread *was* his Body." But quoting Jesus here, repeating his very words in the present tense, and marking the words off with a slight bow of the body—all this has a striking effect. We sense that the past event completely defines the present event as well, the present moment of this liturgy. Over the bread which the people have brought, the priest says Christ's words: "Take this, all of you, and eat of it, / for this is my Body, / which will be given up for you." Then the priest falls silent, and the attention of all the people is fixed on the conse-crated bread as in silence he holds it up before them. He holds it up for the people to see, for them to gaze on it in contemplation. But he like-wise holds it up before God the Father before whom this story is ulti-mately being recounted. After this, he genuflects before the Lord's Body in adoration, and this gesture expresses the whole Church's faith concerning what has happened in this moment. Our plea for the Spirit to come and transform our gifts has been answered in the course of this telling, with the saying again of the words of Jesus.

Something similar occurs with the wine. The priest tells how after the supper Jesus took "this precious chalice." As he recounts this, he picks up the chalice prepared with the wine, which the people have brought that day and into which a little bit of water has been mixed. He continues his narration in a way similar to his narration concern-ing the bread. When he comes to the words of Jesus over the chalice, he again bows slightly and speaks the words in the present tense: "This

IS THE CHALICE OF MY BLOOD." The effect is the same. Silently the chalice is held up before the people and before the Father. Again, the priest genuflects in adoration because the Spirit has come, and with the saying of the words of Jesus, the wine has been transformed into the Blood of Christ.

So much for a careful description of the ritual words and action. They already tell much. But we need also to make some attempt to ponder some of the dimensions of this inexhaustible mystery, this inexhaustible concrete something. We know that together with the epiclesis this narrative accomplishes the transformation of the gifts we have brought. What Jesus did at the Last Supper—and what he still does now in this moment, for this is an Hour that does not pass away—was to set in motion the mighty events that would be the culmination of his life. He was giving his disciples a sign together with a command to repeat it in his memory. This sign would reveal the meaning of his Death, which he knew he would undergo on the morrow. The actual events surrounding his Death and the long hours during which it was stretched out were too terrible to be understood by anyone, perhaps even by the one who was undergoing them. But with this sign performed before and repeated after, Jesus was revealing the meaning of his Death and that he was willingly submitting to it.

Three things at least are striking to us in the sign that Jesus made during this supper the night before he died. First, his use of bread and wine and the context of a meal. He is using these basic symbols of human life together—symbols of love, desire, communion; and he is declaring them to be his voluntary Death. What is Death for him is meant to be nourishment (bread) for us. What is Death for him is even feast (wine) for us. This is a completely unexpected understanding of his Death, and we could never have arrived at it on our own initiative. He is our master and teacher and is instructing us as he gives us this sign.

Not only are these basic symbols of human life, but they have a specific meaning in the context of Jewish Passover, the feast in which

Israel remembered before God His greatest saving deeds in the Exodus. The food and drink of this meal were the language with which the story of Israel's Passover was told. Jesus, the Jew, draws on all its images the night before he dies when, in the context of the Passover meal, he consciously and intentionally summarizes or recapitulates all of Israel's history in himself. In the signs of the meal that he selects, he is conscious that he holds all of Israel and all her history in his hands as he takes up bread and wine, and he identifies that whole history with himself and with the Death he will undergo on the morrow, saying over it, "This is my Body, this is my Blood." This moment, this action, is unfathomably profound. This is not some vague identification of Israel's history with the story of Jesus. It is a sign unmistakable in its significance: Israel's history finds its fulfillment in the Body that will hang on the cross, in the Blood that will be shed there. This Blood opens a new covenant, "the new covenant in my Blood." In short, Jesus, holding the whole history of Israel in his hands, declares it to be his voluntary Death. All the Law and the prophets pointed to this.

The second thing that is striking in the sign that Jesus made is the language he uses. We can certainly call it sacrificial language, even if the word *sacrifice* does not appear. His is "a Body handed over." His is "Blood poured out" to establish a "new and eternal covenant." The repetition of this sign and Jesus' words around it certainly prepare the way for the Church to understand the Eucharist and the Death of Jesus as a sacrifice. The mystery is very dense at this point. As the Church continues to celebrate the Eucharist through her first generations, she eventually comes to understand that Christ's Death is in fact *the* sacrifice against which all others are measured and consequently eclipsed. And the Eucharist that remembers his Death becomes the same sacrifice. There can be no other.

A third thing that is striking in the sign that Jesus made is how it works, how it functions as sign. We are accustomed to calling the Mass a sacrifice. We often use the phrase "the sacrifice of the Mass."

Catholics know—however vaguely—that somehow Christ's sacrifice on Calvary is present at Mass, and this notion is especially associated with the institution narrative. But it is possible to understand something of how this works, of what this means. The institution narrative remembers and enacts the supper on the night before Jesus died. It does not enact the scenes on Calvary. But this supper pointed to the meaning of the Cross, whose meaning is finally revealed in the Resurrection and the rest of the unfolding of the Paschal Mystery. Thus, to remember the supper, which by pre-figuring his Death already was swept up in its hour, is our way of remembering his Death; for the supper now *"re*-figures" for us that hour and is thereby swept up in it. Henceforth, all memorial, all liturgical remembering refers to this central event of salvation history. All remembering is ultimately a remembering of this. The risen presence of the crucified one is the eternally present fact of the new creation, the new covenant. In this sense the sacrifice of Calvary is present and re-presented in the transformed bread and wine which have become the Body and Blood of Christ. The "technique" of memorial splices us into this *fact*.

Throughout all this action and the accompanying words, it remains important for us to remember with attention that it all happens with the bread and wine that we brought; for this is how our communion in the one sacrifice of Christ is accomplished. In effect, by means of our bread and wine our lives are taken up into the one and only story in which the history of the world finds its meaning and fulfillment, the Death and Resurrection of Christ. It is our lives over which Jesus' once pronounced words continue to be pronounced. And it is under these words, under this blessing, that our lives are transformed, and are allowed to become, and to declare his voluntary Death, his sacrifice. In a sermon in the fifth century, Saint Leo the Great managed to express this in a succinct formula: "Sharing the Body and Blood of Christ causes nothing less than our passing over into what we receive, and then in spirit and in flesh we carry him everywhere, the one in whom we were dead, buried and rose again" (Sermon 63, 7).

It is part of our method always to take note of the direction in which any given moment in the liturgy is moving, and we have already observed that our words and actions are directed to God the Father. That the priest speaks and acts in the name of us all is an image of our coming to the Father through Christ. The Holy Spirit shapes and supports our prayer. But even while we are moving toward the Father with our prayer, He is already coming to us, answering our prayer immediately by sending the Spirit and by sending the Son. At this point in the liturgy we are completely immersed in the mystery of the Holy Trinity and the movement of love which continuously flows among Father, Son, and Holy Spirit. The movement is in both directions at once—we toward the Father and the Father toward us!

The Mystery of Faith

After the priest has genuflected in adoration before the Blood of Christ present in the consecrated chalice, he sings or says solemnly the words, "The mystery of faith." This is not so much a rubrical instruction like, "Stand up now" or "Start singing." It is an exclamation of awe and wonder and is the supreme moment in the liturgy for using this word *mystery* to which I have already drawn considerable attention. Something is hidden under the appearances of bread and wine. Faith perceives it. As if in answer to the priest's exclamation, the voice of the assembly rings out declaring what is perceived: "We proclaim your Death, O Lord, / and profess your Resurrection / until you come again." This is an extremely condensed expression of the whole story of salvation. We have said again and again that this is its center, and in the Eucharistic Prayer we concentrate on its center.

There are other possible responses with which the assembly may answer the priest's exclamation. In all of them we are announcing what is hidden under the appearance of the bread and wine. We should be aware that each of the possible formulas is a condensed expression of the center of our salvation and mentions the *past* event of Jesus' Death, the *present* reality of his Resurrection, and his *future* coming in glory. All of that—past, present, and future—is hidden in what lies on the altar, and faith perceives it and proclaims it.

The Memorial (the Anamnesis) and the Offering

What the people express in the condensed formula of the mystery of faith anticipates what the priest says and does next. The last words of Jesus, which he had pronounced over the chalice of wine were, "Do this in memory of me." The Greek word in this text is *anamnesis*, and, similar to the word *epiclesis*, it has long been used as a technical liturgical term designating a particular part of the Eucharistic Prayer. The anamnesis is this part that we are beginning now, and the word literally means "a memorial." Insofar as the whole Eucharistic Prayer has a narrative strand that runs through it, it is all memorial or anamnesis. In a stricter sense, the anamnesis is this prayer that follows the proclamation of the Mystery of Faith.

So, we have heard the Lord's command, "Do this in memory of me." The prayer the priest now begins explicitly states before the Father that we are doing exactly that. In all four of the Eucharistic Prayers, this part of the prayer begins with a "therefore," and it is as important as the "therefore," that introduced the epiclesis. In the epiclesis we dared to ask for the Spirit to transform our gifts *because* it was God's own plan that a perfect offering be made to the glory of His name. Now we pray as we do *because* Jesus said, "Do this in memory of me." The "do this" refers to what we are doing now with the transformed bread and wine. The "in memory of me" refers to his Death and Resurrection. As one of the formulas for the mystery of faith has it, quoting Saint Paul, "When we eat this Bread and drink this Cup, ["do this"] / we proclaim your Death, O Lord, ["in memory of me"] / until you come again."

In reflecting on the fact that the words of Jesus are pronounced over the bread and wine that we brought, I drew a strong conclusion— or rather I explained a conclusion that the Church herself has long drawn from this fact. I said that Jesus declares our lives to be his voluntary Death, his sacrifice. The prayer the priest prays now presumes that this has been accomplished. And because it has been, while the Church remembers Jesus, she also offers to the Father his Body and Blood to which she has been joined. These are the two dimensions of the prayer: memorial and offering.

We are not inert matter in the hands of Jesus or for the action of the Spirit. A marvelous cooperation is occurring in which Jesus, the Spirit, and the worshipping community—the Church—all play a role. We are given the privilege of ourselves offering what Jesus once offered and—it must continually be repeated—which does not pass away. Christ the priest associates his priestly people with him in his offering. To make it clear that there are not two different sacrifices being offered, Jesus' and the Church's, we speak words to the Father in our offering expressing our consciousness that there is only one sacrifice, only one perfect offering. And so we remember: *memores, igitur, Domine . . . ,* "therefore, remembering, O Lord . . . ." It is necessary to recall precisely here what we have said many times: that in the Christian dispensation "remembering" is not a weak calling to mind of a past event. To remember an event of God is itself an event, the event remembered. More than ever, that is the case now. And so we remember the Death of Jesus, his Resurrection, his Ascension. We stand ready to greet him when he comes again in glory. And from this place, inside these events that never pass away, we say to the Father, "we offer you in thanksgiving / this holy and living sacrifice." That *we* offer it is our communion in the sacrifice of Christ, our share in his priesthood. This moment and this place in which we stand is the fulfillment of the Father's plan that "a pure sacrifice may be offered to [His] name." We dared to ask for the Holy Spirit to enable us to make such an offering because it was His plan. In our communion with Christ's Death and Resurrection remembered now, we are able to do so.

CALLING DOWN THE SPIRIT AGAIN— THE SECOND EPICLESIS

Yet the prayer does not stop there. There is a risk that on the level of sign the bread and wine might remain too exterior to ourselves, something that we could handle at arm's length, as it were, as if it were enough somehow to have Christ's sacrifice, however mysteriously, objectively present under the appearances of the bread and wine lying on the altar and say the right words of offering them up to the Father. In fact, the whole rite envisions our eventually consuming the Lord's Body and Blood. The next part of the Eucharistic Prayer anticipates this ritual action and makes an urgent plea that what it means come to pass in us. Using now a strong cultic language of sacrifice, we ask the Father to "Look, we pray, upon the oblation of your Church / and, recognizing the sacrificial Victim . . . ." We stretch out, as it were, this moment of offering before the Father, knowing that the offering— Christ's Body and Blood—will be the basis on which the petition that follows is made: "grant that we, who are nourished / by the Body and Blood of your Son / and filled with his Holy Spirit, / may become one body, one spirit in Christ." This is the second epiclesis, a second request for the Holy Spirit, this time not that the gifts be transformed into the Body and Blood of Christ but that we who receive them be transformed into these. This is our communion with Christ's sacrifice. It will be accomplished in our reception of his Body and Blood. We become his body, not statically, but his body in the form or with the shape of sacrifice. So the plea continues: "May he make of us / an eternal offering to you." This is what Saint Paul had said: "I urge you, *therefore*, by the mercies of God to offer your bodies as a living sacrifice, holy and pleasing to God, your spiritual worship" (Romans 12:1). This is what Saint Augustine had said in speaking of the same: " . . . the whole assembly and community of the saints is offered as a universal sacrifice to God through the High Priest who offered himself . . . " (*City of God*, 10, 6).

Just as there was much to reflect upon in the institution narrative and Consecration—I called these an inexhaustible mystery—so there is in the epiclesis. I have drawn attention to two invocations to the Father to send the Spirit, the first to transform the gifts and the second to transform those who receive the gifts. In reality these are two dimensions of a single request for the Holy Spirit. The transformation of the bread and wine into the Body and Blood of Christ is for our sake. The risen Lord does not somehow personally profit from this remarkable transformation. Such a transformation would have no sense without its reference to us. The Lord becomes bodily present in sacramental form so that the Church can be formed as his body. Putting it this way does not take something from Christ and concentrate the attention on us. Christ is entirely present and adored in the sacramental species, but remembering that he is there for our transformation into his body is a way of acknowledging and facing up fully to all that the Father intends in giving us His beloved Son. It is following faithfully what Jesus himself had indicated as his purpose and whose very words have just been solemnly pronounced in the course of the institution narrative: "FOR THIS IS MY BODY, / WHICH WILL BE GIVEN UP FOR YOU," and, " . . . MY BLOOD . . . / WHICH WILL BE POURED OUT FOR YOU . . . ." This is our strongest warrant for daring to ask for so much and for daring to believe that we receive it. "Father," Jesus had prayed at the supper the night before he died, "Father, I pray that all may be one as you, Father, are in me, and I in you; I pray that they may be one in us. I have given them the glory you gave me that they may be one, as we are one" (John 17:21–22). So, what happens at Mass at this point? Christ converges bodily on his Church, with the Holy Spirit coming out everywhere from him, to make the Church his body. The scope of the transformation is not that Christ be trapped in the Eucharistic species but that he be extended bodily to his Church.

STEPPING BACK A MINUTE AND COLLECTING OUR THOUGHTS

I want to pause a moment in our moving through the various parts of the Eucharistic Prayer, to pause and reflect a little beyond the immediate meaning of each part. Perhaps the reader will have noticed a practical problem in what I am saying; namely, that it is too beautiful. It would be nice were it all so, but our experience in the day-to-day repudiates all these glorious claims. Sunday by Sunday all of us are repeatedly nourished by his Body and Blood, but often evidence is scant that we are thereby filled with his Holy Spirit, and more scant still that we have become one body, one spirit in Christ. So, does anything at all really happen at Mass? This is a very real question and a fair one. It is not solved by a simple exhortation or scolding, something to the effect of firmly reminding all involved that we ought to live the realities of the Mass. Of course that is true and should be taken very seriously. But perhaps even with our best efforts to do so, we will fall short of being spontaneously described as "filled with the Holy Spirit" and "one body in Christ." Yet I think we can gain some understanding (though not a resolution) of the disturbing paradox by reflecting for a moment on what happens to time during the course of our prayer. Here is a deep mystery. Let us try to enter it.

If talk about anamnesis inevitably has about it a certain pull to the past, to a memory of the deeds of Jesus in history, then talk about epiclesis and the work of the Spirit—would that we could say it all at the same time!—clearly shows that "remembering Jesus" includes the paradox of remembering a future. Indeed, the Spirit pulls the weight of memory as much, if not more so, to the future as to the past. For there is only one way to remember Jesus crucified and to encounter him or, as the Latin tradition has long loved to consider the Eucharist, only one way to have the sacrifice of Calvary present on the altar: Jesus crucified is none other than the now risen Lord, present to us in the Spirit. And the risen Lord, freed from the bondage of time and space, even while being present in all time and space, is already living the future that is the recapitulation of all things in himself (cf. Ephesians 1:10). It is this Lord, a Lord already established in his future, who is present to the Church that celebrates his memorial. Among the things hidden in the mystery of the Eucharist is this already accomplished future, and we mysteriously enter it already as we celebrate.

The salvation that Christianity proclaims is not salvation *from* the world and its history but the salvation of the world itself and its history. This distinguishes Christian faith from other world religions. Said liturgically, nothing like the Eucharist happens in any other ritual of any other religion. Yet the fullest dimensions of this claim can only be understood by our referring to what happens in the Eucharistic celebration when the Holy Spirit is invoked. For a huge problem remains in the experience of the whole world, even in the world of those who celebrate Eucharist; namely, the horror of the present historical situation. This horror is the experience of every generation. It is precisely for this reason that the Church learned that she must continually invoke the Holy Spirit in her prayer. The salvation of the world has not been promised solely *within* history; it is also posited *beyond* it in the definitive future of the kingdom of heaven. The epiclesis, which transforms the assembly into the body of Christ, is a visit of the Spirit from the future. The Spirit creates of the worshipping community not so much an icon of the community as it is in its present historical circumstances but as it shall be.

This can perhaps be grasped with the help of an image. I think of a plant or a tree whose roots stretch out to both past and future but whose head springs up in the present. Without its nourishment from the future, this plant could not survive; and yet the plant we see in the present indicates that the Church's liturgical experience of the future has its effects on the present. Experience shows—and the epiclesis reveals the theological reasons for it—that the union and communion of all peoples in Christ, and indeed of the whole cosmos in him, cannot be achieved merely by human efforts historically conceived. Human attempts at togetherness, even those informed by what is known of Christ from history, can never accomplish the communion in Trinitarian life to which God would bring the whole creation. The epiclesis reveals that this communion—which is God's final goal— must penetrate history now also from the future. This absolute need for the future shows why the kingdom of God can never be simply identified with history as such. It is not a conquest of the world as we know it. It is the world as it is known in the Eucharistic celebration.

THE INTERCESSIONS

There is a striking ecclesial dimension to what is asked for in the two-pronged epiclesis. That is to say, we should not be thinking only of ourselves as individuals or only of ourselves as this particular assembly becoming one body with Christ. The very logic of what we are asking for demands that we understand that we are being joined in communion with the whole Church across the world and across the centuries. This awareness expresses itself in the intercessions that now follow. Like the huge intercession for this gift of the Holy Spirit, we make these intercessions also on the basis of and in the presence of the sacrifice stretched out now before the Father.

We said that there is a sense in which *anamnesis* at one and the same time refers to a dimension of the whole Eucharistic Prayer (its narrative dimension) and to a specific part (that part immediately following the Consecration). Something similar is true of epiclesis. In its broad sense *epiclesis* refers to all the elements of intercession contained in the whole prayer, while in a more precise sense it refers to the specific pleas for the Holy Spirit. There is a profound relationship between these two dimensions. Remembering what God has done (anamnesis), we have confidence that He will answer our intercessions now (epiclesis). Stretching out before the Father the sacrifice of Christ (anamnesis), we ask (epiclesis).

In the requests of each of the two parts of the epiclesis there is a concentration on what is immediately before us. We pray that the bread and wine on this altar be transformed into the Body and Blood of Christ. We pray that those of us in this assembly may become one body in Christ. Now we pray that all this may be extended beyond those immediately present in this assembly. Those present could be called the visible icon of "the whole redeemed city" (to use Saint Augustine's phrase again), which as such is invisible to the given community but nonetheless present. The words that follow acknowledge this, pray that it be so, render us aware of a presence not visible to our eyes.

Each of the four Eucharistic Prayers expresses these intercessions in different ways, but they are different ways of praying for the same thing. I will speak here about what is common to all of them. One of the things to note in these intercessions is that specific names are mentioned. We need to develop a greater sensitivity to what a beautiful practice this is. There are first of all the names of saints in heaven. In the first place among these is Mary, the Mother of God, then Peter and Paul and the other apostles, then the martyrs, and finally all the saints. Of course, we cannot actually name them all, but all of them are present, and naming some is designed to make us aware of the presence of all. We also name the present pope and our bishop. In doing this, we are not simply deciding to pray for them because they have a rough job. Rather, the whole local church is named in the person of the bishop, and the communion of the local church with all the other churches throughout the world is named in the person of the bishop of Rome, the pope. So, again, though we cannot name every member of the Church throughout the world, all are mysteriously present, and the naming of pope and bishop is designed to make us aware of their presence. We also name, not one by one but as a whole, everybody in the world, meaning those who do not know Christ or those who refuse to believe in him. We pray, "May this sacrifice of our reconciliation . . . / advance the peace and salvation of all the world." We name before the Father "all who seek you with a sincere heart." We also name the dead. It is a relief to our love and sense of loss to name particular loved ones who have died. In some Masses some can be named aloud, others in our hearts; but in the end we mean to name before God all the innumerable dead.

I speak of developing a greater sensitivity to pronouncing these names. Throughout biblical revelation God has taught us how marvelous a mystery is a person's name. The mystery of our names is rooted in the mystery of God's own name: Father, Son, and Holy Spirit. Having a name means that someone can call to me. God gives me a name by calling me into existence, and our names for one another echo this gift. In fact, I don't even know that I am an *I* until another person says my name to me and I respond with the *You* uniquely held in the name of the one calling. Thus a name is a little song in which a person's whole being is embodied. To say the name is a little mystery, a little concrete sound, which renders the other present. Throughout the course of this prayer we have been saying the name of God again and again—Father, Son, and Holy Spirit. Now we say all our names also. This is the liturgical shape of what we observed in the Creed: that we cannot name Father, Son, and Holy Spirit in the abstract, but we must also name the Church. The Church is not abstract either. She is all these persons, each with a name. In the Church we all call to one another by name.

So, naming is a fundamental characteristic of these intercessions. What do we ask for when we name? There are two ways in which we can understand it. The first is to note that the formulation of the prayers often asks God to "remember" all these whom we name. This can seem odd. Has God forgotten? Does He need our reminding? Obviously this cannot be the sense of "remember" in these prayers. Rather, it carries the specific sense we saw in liturgical anamnesis. It is by remembering the deeds of God that His saving deeds from the past become present to us. When we remember, God can and will be active for us now. We call this His remembering, and we ask for it. We remember the events by which He saved us, and we ask God to remember. When we remember other people and ask God to remember them, we are asking for something similar. We are asking that the others not vanish from us into the separating recesses of time, distance, and death. Only God can make us united as one across what would otherwise be such a huge divide.

A second way in which we can understand what we are asking for in these intercessions is to recall that they are an extension of our precise epiclesis. We asked for the Spirit to transform this bread and wine and to unite into one body all who are nourished by this. Now we are simply extending that request and thereby expressing our desire to be one body in Christ with all those whom we have named—with all the saints, with the Church across the whole world, with all the dead, with all people everywhere.

What happens at Mass when we say these names before the Father with our sacrifice spread out before Him? All those named become present to us because God remembers them in response to what our sacrifice asks. We enter already into our future where we will be perfectly joined together as one body in Christ.

This colossal prayer moves now toward its climax. It has remembered Christ's sacrifice and, by remembering, rendered it present as the event that defines the present action. It has prayed that we be joined in communion with this sacrifice, that we become one body with Christ's body, together with the people of God across time and across space. With all this "in place," we make a huge final thrust with our prayer toward the future we hope for in Christ, a future which we feel already invading the present moment of our prayer. Meaning all the living and dead with whom we are now in communion, we say "we"; and speaking for all we say to the Father, "There (in heaven) we hope to enjoy for ever the fullness of your glory, / through Christ our Lord." Such eternal enjoyment could be described, of course, as communion with the Father. But we should not fail to notice the plural form, the "we." Communion with the Father is something that we can only enjoy in communion with one another. Communion with one another is not communion of a lesser order, second to that of communion with God. Communion with one another is an essential part of God's plan; and having designed salvation with this shape, God surely is teaching us and causing us to participate in the tremendous regard He has for us, His tremendous love toward us. We are made for this double communion. Saint Augustine expresses it with utter precision, when he says, "The true peace of rational creatures, which is the only peace of the heavenly city, consists in a perfectly ordered and harmonious enjoyment of God and of one another in God" (*City of God* 19, 17).

Glorifying God (Doxology) and the Great Amen

Enjoyment of God and of one another in God—this enjoyment is already tasted in the Eucharistic feast. Another name for this is praise. There is also a technical term, based on Greek like the others, for this dimension of the Eucharistic Prayer. It is called *doxology*. A sense of doxology or praising and glorifying God has run through the Eucharistic Prayer from the very start. In fact, in the Preface and the *Sanctus* (Holy, Holy, Holy) the notion of doxology was very much to the fore, even if I did not use this technical term yet. But there is also a specific part of the Eucharistic Prayer that is called the doxology, and it is this that closes the whole prayer. Doxology is this prayer's final thrust, come full circle from the doxology of the Preface.

The bishop lifts up the bread and wine—bread and wine which we have brought, bread and wine transformed into the Body and Blood of Christ in the form of his sacrifice which never passes away, bread and wine which we are shortly to consume—and lifting them up he presents them to God the Father as the "pure sacrifice . . . offered to [His] name." "Through him, and with him, and in him, / O God, almighty Father, / in the unity of the Holy Spirit, / all glory and honor is yours, / for ever and ever." In that moment the Church is doing what Christ did and forever does: she offers his one body, to which she has been joined, to the Father for the glory of His name and for the salvation of the world. This is our communion in the sacrifice of Christ. This is perfect praise.

The Trinitarian shape of this final doxology cannot, of course, be missed. If from the start of the Eucharistic Prayer every bit of it is directed to God the Father, now this is the finale of what is directed to Him. If until now we were always conscious of being able to come to the Father only *through* Christ, now in the finale we pile up the prepositions in enjoyment of every conceivable direction and dimension of his mediation. We pound the point in exultation: *through* him, and *with* him, and *in* him—this is the only course along which we could come to God the Father. And if throughout the prayer we were conscious that with every "*through* Christ" there is an "*in* the Holy Spirit," now in the finale we add a word to the Spirit's role, which characterizes the person of the Spirit within the divine Trinity as well as the Spirit's work in us: we say "in the unity of the Holy Spirit." We see here how praise (doxology) is the perfect summary for what we have remembered (anamnesis) and what we have asked for (epiclesis). This is always the full shape of Christian prayer. Remembering what God has done, we ask Him for what we desire, and we finish by praising Him.

Words and gestures together—the bishop or the priest holds up the Body and Blood of Christ, to which we are all united, and offers these to the Father in order to give Him glory and honor. The direction of movement is clear. The whole world is coming toward the Father through Christ, and this is likewise the work of the Church. We would not be wrong to think of the Father as being overwhelmed by what He sees coming toward Him. He sees His Son coming and the whole world reconciled to Him in the Body of His Son. I know it sounds odd to speak of overwhelming God, but much of what is revealed to us of God in Christ unsettles abstract notions of the deity. How else are we to take the full measure of what is happening in this moment of the final doxology? The Father has given His Son to the world. In his sacrifice on the Cross the Son destroys in his own body the sins of us all. Now in that same body, risen from the dead, he brings us all as one body before his Father and says, "This is for your glory and honor!" The Father sees His Son in the only way that He can see him; that is, clothed in our flesh, in his crucified and now risen Body. In seeing His Son, He sees us as well, for there is no other Son but the whole Son. The Father exclaims, "Beloved Son, in whom I am well pleased!" The whole world is reconciled to God. This is what happens at Mass. We are standing in our definitive future.

The bishop or priest has led this whole prayer, speaking in the name of the Church, acting in the person of Christ. The assembly experiences through his leadership the indispensable mediation of Christ. It has followed Christ through the memorial of his Death and Resurrection and arrives with him in the presence of the Father. To all that Christ has done, to all that is happening, the assembly cries out a resounding Amen. This is the biggest Amen of the Mass and so is the biggest Amen in the world. We have, as it were, warmed up for this one by saying it earlier in the liturgy at important junctures. This Amen contains all others. This is the fullest sense of the Amen I spoke of which concludes the Creed. Now we have all the articles of the

Creed—Father, Son, and Holy Spirit believed in the Church—as event. And the Amen that agrees to it, understands something of it, desires it to be so—this is an Amen echoing round the globe, echoing through the centuries, echoing in the halls of heaven. This Amen never ends. In the Mass, from our own place and time, we are spliced into this eternal Amen, and we shall sing forever what we are singing now. Amen!

Chapter Six

Communion

After the great Amen that closes the Eucharistic Prayer, the whole assembly is on its feet because it has been carried by this prayer into the very presence of God and into its future in Christ. The congregation assembled before the altar with its priest at the center is a mystery. Hidden in this image is the assembly standing with Christ in heaven before the throne of God. Now begins yet another unit of the Mass, called as a whole the Communion Rite. What is happening here? What is revealed now? We can answer—we must answer—with an answer that seems too easy, that seems to say too much and too little. But we must say it and try to give it its concrete content. The answer is: Love. Love is happening; Love is now revealed. Love is communion.

The Church's experience of communion in the Eucharistic celebration has taught her that love cannot be defined in just any old way and certainly not in a worldly way; that is, by taking human love between individuals as a starting point, a starting point from which one might make a comparison with God's love, saying something to the effect of, "God's love is like that." For the Christian, schooled in this moment of the liturgy, love is not like anything. Love *is* what is happening now. What love is, is revealed by God here and now. If anything, human love is like God's love in that it has its source in God and is at best some reflection of it. All love is defined, true and divine love is revealed here at this point in the celebration. The Church is now standing within the one love of the Father, Son, and Holy Spirit. This divine Trinitarian love has a form, a shape, a dynamic; and it is all revealed in what is possible for the Church in this moment. All that follows in the Communion Rite is what is possible for the Church now.

It begins with the Lord's Prayer. The Lord's Prayer—the Lord's own way of praying—is possible for the Church now. Through the priest's exhortation, Christ invites his body to address the words of a prayer to his Father. This exhortation and prayer open the next and final major liturgical unit of the Mass. It extends from the Lord's Prayer all the way through to the Prayer after Communion. There are a number of elements to this unit, and we will look at them each in turn. There is, first, the Lord's Prayer, then the Rite of Peace, the Breaking of the Bread, the distribution and reception of Communion, and lastly the Prayer after Communion. All of these elements taken together are called the Communion Rite. The climax of the unit is our eating and drinking, a ritual action which effectively accomplishes our communion, our participation, in the sacrifice of Christ which has been offered to the Father in the Eucharistic Prayer. To speak with the technical language that an anthropologist might use for understanding sacrifice, it is the *consummation* of the sacrifice. Even with ancient animal sacrifices there was always this element. The sacrifice is directed toward God; in its consummation those who offer it are joined to God. The same happens here but in a way that is unique to the Christian realities. If I may state the case bluntly: in the Communion Rite we swallow everything that has lain on the altar during the Eucharistic Prayer.

To understand all the elements of this unit it can be useful to think in terms of words and actions. First there are the *words* of the Lord's Prayer and then *actions* which quite literally en-act what has been said and implied in words. So, first I will comment on the *words* of the prayer and their significance in this context. Then I will comment on the *actions* which accomplish and correspond to what has been asked for in the prayer.

The Lord's Prayer

There is a precise reason why the Lord's Prayer is recited at this moment. Its recitation here is the foundation of any other praying of this prayer throughout our Christian lives. Here its original and fullest meaning is revealed and defined. In our discussion of the doxology which concluded the Eucharistic Prayer, we saw in effect that by the sacrifice of Christ we have been thrust into the very heart of the Father and thrust into our definitive future with God. The offering of Christ's sacrifice to the Father climaxes with the words,"O God, almighty Father . . . / all glory and honor is yours, / for ever and ever." And now the Communion Rite begins with the words "Our Father." Let us think about how much happens in this. I will comment on the prayer phrase by phrase.

Father

We begin with the joyous invocation of God by a name that it is possible for us to call Him only through our communion in the sacrifice of Christ: the name "Father." With this invocation on his lips, Jesus breathed his last: "Father, into your hands I commend my spirit" (Luke 23:46). Empowered by the Spirit, we cry out together with Jesus this name that never ceases to sound from the place of the cross. In this invocation there is contained all that humanity desires and all that it was made for. And our invocation will receive a response, the same response that Jesus received and forever receives. It is his name uttered back by the Father: "Beloved Son, in whom I am well pleased" (Matthew 3:17; 17:5; Mark 1:11; Luke 3:22). This becomes our name as well, for we have been established in communion with Christ's sacrifice, recapitulated now in this exchange of names. This exchange of names is not merely the sound of vocables flying between heaven and earth. Rather, it is an action. If the action of Jesus' Death is recapitulated in the name "Father" cried out by him, the name "Son" is enacted in the Father's raising Jesus from the dead. This is as the psalmist mysteriously prophesied and as the apostle Paul once preached: "You are my beloved son. Today I have begotten you" (see Acts 13:33; Hebrews 1:5; referring to Psalms 2:7). That the eternal Son might share his name with us—this is what he is so anxious for as soon as he rises from the dead. He tells Mary Magdalene with urgency, "Go to my brothers and tell them, 'I am ascending to my Father and your Father, to my God and your God'" (John 20:17. See also Matthew 28:10).

I have mentioned a number of times that by means of the Eucharistic liturgy we are mysteriously thrust into the future and do our praying there. The intensity of this experience grows in the Communion Rite and can be detected already in the experience of saying "Father" in this prayer. In the future, when everything in heaven and on earth is recapitulated in Christ, all creation will be privileged to address its Source with the intimacy and affection that have been the Son's and the Spirit's from all eternity. Father is a name that names Him as Source and Font, but likewise a name in which our own relation to Him is expressed, a name of love and intimacy. It is the human name for the One from whom the divine Word has eternally come forth. Now we say this name with him. This is communion. This is Love.

Sometimes nowadays it is said that the name "Father" for God gives too strong a masculine image for our understanding of God and so should be eliminated or at least used alongside feminine names and images as well. Of course God is neither a he nor a she, and so no name and no number of rightly balanced feminine and masculine names can in themselves ever express who God is. But we Christians know God and address ourselves to God in the way that Jesus taught us. When Jesus teaches us the name "Father" for our most intimate address to God—in imitation of his own—we have just one more instance of the miracle of Christ's incarnation, the miracle in which finite, limited forms are made capable of bearing infinite divine realities. The finite, limited form—in this case the name "Father"—bends under the weight of the divine reality it carries and is re-defined beyond its limitations. If *Father* were a term of our own invention for God, then it could be justifiably complained that it is hopelessly lopsided and limits God to masculine categories, that it runs the risk of simply evoking the deficiencies of particular, earthly, failed, and bad fathers. But in the mouth of the eternal Word become flesh, "Father" is the finite, limited name he gave us, which is a gate through which we pass into an infinite reality; namely, his own loving relation to the Source from which he himself is eternally begotten.

Our

This "our" is first of all the "our" of the Son and Spirit. The total and infinite love exchanged in the dialogue between Father and Son from all eternity is known, experienced, acknowledged, enjoyed, and honored by another—the Spirit—who proceeds from the Father, from the Father who ever begets a Son, who ever utters a Word. This is Love.

Love is a Father who ever utters His Word. This Word has become flesh, and so now if he says "Father," it is from his flesh that he does so. And the Spirit is present at this utterance, knowing it, acknowledging it, enjoying it, and honoring it. The sacrifice of Christ offered in the Eucharistic Prayer has purchased for us adoption into this love. As the first manifestation of this adoption, the Church cries out with the Son and with the Holy Spirit, "Our Father!" So this "our" is the original and eternal "our" of the Son and Spirit, but in a marvelous cooperation we are made capable—always by the transformation of the gifts that we brought—of saying "our" together with the Son and the Spirit, indeed on the same level with them. We are not vaguely addressing ourselves to God as a "whoever is up there." We are personally addressing the one whom Jesus addressed as Father and whom he revealed by so addressing. The sacrifice of Christ was Blood shed to establish a "new and eternal covenant"; that is, we become *God's* people and He is *"our"* God.

Finally, in the most obvious sense the "our" refers to all of us—however many, however few—present at any given celebration. But when we notice the origins of this "our" in the eternal Son and eternal

Spirit, we are likewise made sensitive to the fact that it is not just this particular assembly that speaks with the Son and the Spirit to the Father. This "our" is the our of the future, and it refers to our particular assembly standing together with all people who have ever lived and who ever will live. It is the "our" that the angels also address together to their Source. It is also us as human beings giving voice to the whole cosmos that "awaits with eager longing" (Romans 8:19) precisely this priestly service from us. This is another reason why this part of the rite is called Communion. It is the biggest "our" imaginable. It embraces everybody and everything.

Who art in heaven

It is Jesus who taught us this prayer and who prays it in an original, radical way. It is he who prays it within us. Praying with him we learn that heaven is not so much a place as it is a way of being. When we say, "who art in heaven," we don't mean "who art elsewhere"; rather, we are acknowledging in our divine Father His majesty and His sovereignty over the whole material order and the whole course of human history. His is a way of being before the beginning of creation, and it will be His way of being after the end of time. Heaven is the "place" of our future, where we are destined to share forever in God's way of being. Another name for this way of being is communion, for God's way of being is that God is Father, Son, and Holy Spirit, Love moving in an eternal flow. When we pray this prayer and acknowledge a Father in heaven, we are already there where we are meant to forever be, within Love's eternal flow. Paradoxically, then, in this moment heaven is revealed as interior to us rather than somehow hopelessly beyond us. And yet heaven placed within us is not our own doing and not a part of our original nature. It is placed within us when the Father hands us the Body and Blood of His Son as our food and drink. In Christ heaven and earth are joined together forever.

Hallowed be thy name

Here we pray that the name "Father" be known and uttered with reverence everywhere, in all times, in all places, and in the whole creation. But "Father" is a name that unfolds, and this unfolding is also the hallowing of His name. In the name "Father" is contained the mystery of the Son and the Holy Spirit, and now we know—always by means of the transformation of the gifts—that our new name is likewise contained within the divine name. When we pray these words together with Jesus, we enter into his same relationship with the Father. This is as he prayed the night before he died: "Father, I have made your name known to those you gave me out of the world" (John 17:6). Jesus concentrates in these few words—hallowed be thy name—the entire thrust of his being, of his eternal being which is one with his being in the flesh among us. He is eternally grateful to the One from whom he comes forth; he is eternally turned toward him; he does whatever the Father does; he can do nothing by himself (see John 5:19). His whole sacrifice on the cross was an uttering of this petition by his entire body. As we say these words now, we say nothing less; for we have been made part of his entire body.

Thy kingdom come

God's kingdom is His definitive rule manifestly established. It is His surprising and unexpected drawing near to us to save us from sin. It is his decisive victory over sin and death. It is the whole creation and the whole of human history being invaded by the dynamic of Love that God is—Father, Son, and Holy Spirit. This petition of the prayer refers primarily to all this being established in Christ's second coming; but as we have seen, in the Death and Resurrection of Christ, God's kingdom has already come, or perhaps better put, it has been continually coming, in a way that cannot be turned back, from the time when the eternal Word became flesh, when he was crucified and rose from the dead. Our risen Lord in his human body, in his human nature, is already established in his definitive glory; and we pray that he may come from that future to take all things up into it. Jesus' coming again in glory is the Father's kingdom. This prayer in effect is the same as that which closes the entire Bible: "Marana tha! Come, Lord Jesus." In some sense this supplication will already be answered by the Father when in just a short time we receive the Lord's Body and Blood. Indeed, every petition of this prayer is mysteriously answered in our being given that holy food and drink. This is what happens at Mass.

Thy will be done on earth as it is in heaven

In the Eucharistic sacrifice on our altar, we have in fact made a place on earth where the will of God is entirely accomplished and done, just as it is in heaven. In its most radical sense "as it is in heaven" means just as the will of the Father is entirely "done" in the person of the Son and the person of the Spirit, and this before time began. But there is also something that God wills from the beginning of creation, and Sacred Scripture reveals this to us: "God's *will* is that all may be saved and come to knowledge of the truth" (1 Timothy 2:3–4). All in fact can be saved in the sacrifice that has been offered. We pray here that the sacrifice will bear this fruit. Or again, "He has made known to us the mystery of his *will* . . . to recapitulate all things in heaven and on earth in Christ" (Ephesians 1:9–10). We have already used this language to understand what is happening in the transformation of bread and wine, "fruit of the earth and work of human hands." All things are recapitulated in Christ in the sacrifice that lies on our altar. Again, we pray here that the sacrifice will bear this fruit.

In our reception of the Lord's Body and Blood, our own bodies become the place on earth where the will of the Father is done, for our bodies are joined to the one body of Christ in which, as we have just said, heaven and earth are joined together forever. Jesus had said, "I always do what is pleasing to the Father" (John 8:29). Now we pray that we may be joined to him in this. Our reception of Communion will be our acting out of this desire. Yet when we say "on earth," we do not mean merely ourselves; we are praying here for the extension across the whole earth of what we intend and enact around this altar. Being made one body in Christ is another way of saying that we are "saved and come to knowledge of the truth." It is "all things recapitulated in Christ." This is the Father's will. May His will be done!

*   *   *

So far in this prayer all our attention has been focused on the Father for His own sake; our desire has been to glorify Him: "*thy* name . . . / *thy* kingdom . . . / *thy* will . . . ." In this way of praying we know that we are in the presence of God exactly as the divine Son stands in His presence, with all his same energies directed toward his Father. Only in him can we pray this way. This is nothing less than the entire sacrifice of Christ condensed into the first petitions of this prayer. But then the energy and direction of the prayer turn. Its second half reveals the Church in the tension between the future in which it already stands and this present time. So, having prayed in the first half as we can pray in the already present future of the liturgy, we next pray for what we, who have tasted this future, need to live in the present. If we said, "thy, thy, thy" in the first half, now we say, "us, us, us" in the second half, not in a self-centered way but simply expressing our reliance. The "us" or the "we" is as big as the "our" for the opening invocation. We are speaking in communion with all of heaven and in the name of every-one and everything on earth. Thus,

Give us this day our daily bread
In a general way, of course, with this petition we are asking our heav-enly Father for all that we need to stay alive. It expresses our love and trust, our recognition that the Father who gave us life will also give us all that life requires. By asking we acknowledge that everything is received from God; every moment of our existence is from Him; and we do not take it for granted. With affection we ask that He keep us

alive and well. And we ask for this not in some vague way like any tribe might ask its deity for well-being. Our asking is part of a covenant relationship. He is our God, and we are His people. We have already agreed to His offer to take care of us. This is why we ask, confident that we will receive.

Yet there is a lovely second level of meaning in this petition when we say this prayer within the Eucharistic liturgy. With bread and wine lying on the altar transformed into the Lord's Body and Blood, how can we not think of that when we utter the words, "Give us this day our daily bread"? We remember our Lord's teaching that we "cannot live by bread alone . . . but by every word that proceeds from the mouth of God" (Deuteronomy 8:3; Matthew 4:4). So the Word of God received as real food, the Body and Blood of Christ accepted as spiritual nourishment—this is the ultimate "bread" we ask the Father to give to us.

There is also a second level of meaning in the expression "this day," or literally, "today." Whenever the liturgy uses the word *today*, it refers not merely to a particular limited day of mundane time. It refers more basically to a long everlasting day that knows no setting of the sun, the day and the hour of Christ's Resurrection. So in the end we are praying that we may be inside that day and be fed on the Lord's Body and Blood. This is our real bread, our "super-essential" bread, as we would say if we were translating the Greek literally. We ask this not just for ourselves, the members of our particular assembly. The "us" and the "our" of this petition includes everyone, everything.

It is our Father who will give us this bread. This is why in the ritual for actually receiving Communion one of the rules of our ritual's serious play is that we receive the Body and Blood of the Lord from the hands of the priest or from other ministers who for practical reasons help him in the distribution. But the point is we don't just go and pick it up by ourselves. To receive the super-essential bread from the Father is to receive Christ himself, and in the person of the priest Christ himself stands before each of us handing himself over to us. Again, this is the revelation of love. "God so loved the world that he gave his only Son" (John 3:16). As Jesus said, "My Father gives you the true bread from heaven, for the bread of God is that which comes down from heaven and gives life to the world" (John 6:32–33). When those listening to him said to him, "Lord, give us this bread always," he responded, "I myself am the bread of life" (John 6:35).

Forgive us our trespasses as we forgive those who trespass against us
It is normal enough that in prayer we should ask God for the forgiveness of our sins, but what is astonishing in this petition is the condition that we dare to attach to it; namely, that we be forgiven in the way that we forgive. This would be a very dangerous prayer were it not prayed in, and through, and with Christ, as we are doing in the most intense way possible at this moment of the Eucharist. In Christ's sacrifice on the Cross, which lies on our altar as we address these words to God, he forgave those who were putting him to death, praying, "Father, forgive them; they do not know what they are doing" (Luke 23:34). As we pray this petition of the Lord's Prayer, the Father sees us in His Son in this hour that does not pass away. In our communion with his sacrifice, his perfect forgiveness of others is shared with us. We swallow his energy for love and forgiveness and are empowered to love as he did, far beyond what we could ever accomplish on our own. And thus our trespasses will be forgiven not to the measure of our own puny efforts at forgiving others, but to the measure of Christ himself. Of course, we must then live to this measure, truly forgiving as he forgave. But the point is, we can do so only through communion with him, never on our own steam alone.

Clearly, in claiming such complete communion in Christ's own perfect forgiveness of others we are again within the realm of our future state in heaven, already praying inside the heavenly liturgy. Perfect forgiveness of one another and perfect communion with one another is part of the future beatitude of heaven. By tasting it now we can bring its reality into our present.

And lead us not into temptation

We feel again the tension between future and present. Here we are obviously praying with an awareness that we are not entirely and definitively established in the future beatitude to which we are called. So we pray that the fruit of our communion will be, among other things, that God will not allow us to take the way that leads to sin. Even as this present moment of prayer is filled with joy and peace, we still know that when this particular celebration is over we shall be engaged again in the battle between good and evil. Knowing that by ourselves we lack the wisdom and strength to conduct the battle with success, we cast ourselves entirely on our heavenly Father, begging Him to save us from stumbling onto a way that might lead us away from Him. If we are lacking in wisdom and strength, still we are able here to place our hearts and wills in the hands of God, telling Him that we want never to fall away from the communion in which we now stand.

But deliver us from evil

Evil is no abstraction; it is from Satan himself that we ask deliverance, knowing that without the divine assistance we would be in his clutches. He is a liar and a deceiver; he hates us; he is jealous of our life in God; he seeks to destroy God's loving plan of salvation. "The whole world is in the power of the evil one," says the apostle John (1 John 5:19). Our deliverance from him lies in the communion we are about to receive, for in it we are "begotten of God" with the only begotten Son of God. As the same apostle says, "We know that any one begotten of God does not sin, but he who was begotten of God protects him" (1 John 5:18).

Once again it is necessary to be aware of the vast range of this prayer. The "us" is not simply the particular assembly praying. That assembly prays in the name of the whole world, that the whole world be freed from all evils, past, present, and future, that the whole world be freed from Satan, the evil one.

* * *

These are the very words that Jesus taught us to pray, and they could not be more forcefully directed to the Father than in the present moment of the Mass as we prepare to receive the Body and Blood of the Father's Son. The prayer finishes with a cry for deliverance that is at once anguished and filled with hope. In what follows, the prayer's last petition echoes several times before it fades away and gives place to a different prayer. The echo is heard in the voice of the priest who prays alone a kind of expansion of the last petition: "Deliver us, Lord, we pray, from every evil / graciously grant peace in our days, / that, by the help of your mercy, / we may be always free from sin / and safe from all distress . . . ." There is a bright finish to the prayer that exactly names the condition in which we are standing. We are surrounded in our lives by evils and distress, and praying for deliverance from these, "as we await the blessed hope / and the coming of our Savior, Jesus Christ." Our place of prayer is a middle ground: on the one hand, the evils of this world; on the other, the coming of Christ from the future. In this middle ground the whole assembly adds doxology to the priest's expanded petition, a doxology which we can utter precisely because in hope we see our Savior coming. Thus, we conclude our dialogue with the Father, these words of communion with Him, by saying, "For the kingdom, / the power and the glory are yours / now and for ever."

The Rite of Peace

In the next prayer something striking occurs. The priest up to this point in the liturgy has always addressed his words either to the assembly or to God the Father. Now he addresses a prayer directly to Christ. It is a prayer for peace. We can think of *peace* as another word for communion, another name for Christ's Body and Blood that we are about to receive. The prayer recalls our Lord's words at the Last Supper in which he himself in effect calls his Body and Blood by this other name, peace. He said, "I leave you peace, my peace I give you" (John 14:27). These words are part of a long discourse in which on the night before he dies Jesus explains to his apostles the meaning of the Death he is about to undergo. Explaining the same, he had said, "This is my Body, this is my Blood." We have said it in many ways now, and we must remind ourselves of it again here: without the Lord's instruction, without divine assistance, we could not penetrate the mystery of his Death. Hidden in his Death is our peace. Thus, the first thing the risen Lord says to his apostles in appearing to them is, "Peace to you!" (John 20:21). The apostle meditates on this mystery: "For he [Jesus Christ] is our peace . . . that he might create in himself one new person in place of two, thus establishing peace, and might reconcile both with God, in one body, through the cross . . . " (Ephesians 2:14–16), or again: " . . . through him to reconcile all things in himself, making peace by the blood of his cross . . . " (Colossians 1:20). As we prepare to receive his Body and Blood, we address ourselves directly to him and, recalling the peace he once promised, ask him for this same peace in our present and in our future. And we call it by yet another name: unity, "peace and unity / in accordance with your will."

Then the priest greets the assembly with the very words of our risen Lord. "The peace of the Lord be with you always," he says. The assembly answers, "And with your spirit." This is yet another little mystery, in which we experience Christ at the head of his body passing his peace and unity into his whole body. Then the priest directs the people, "Let us offer each other the sign of peace." And all the members of the assembly turn to those immediately near them and offer the same greeting of the risen Lord. This is a ritual exchange, not a practical greeting. It is part of what we have called the serious play of ritual. By means of the set phrase, "Peace be with you," and a gesture which signifies our love for one another in Christ—in the old days this was a sober, stylized embrace—we are playing out (and so experiencing) yet another dimension of communion; namely, our being joined together as one body in Christ. We who have just said together to God, "Our Father," in consequence now turn to one another and say, "Brother" and "Sister." We who have just prayed, "Forgive us as we forgive," turn to one another with this sign of reconciliation among ourselves.

All this is a strong and powerful ritual expression of the love that the members of Christ's body must share among themselves as the condition for being united with their head. It places a sign of reconciliation and peace within the Communion Rite as a whole. We embrace one another in the peace that comes from the sacrifice offered, and at the same time we are making a sign of the reality signified in the sacrament we are about to receive. We have prayed, "Forgive us as we forgive," and now we make a sign of that intention before receiving "our daily bread." When this rite is properly carried out—not allowing it to lose its ritual character and break down into a short chat session, which of course would make no sense here—it has the potential for refusing to let those who are to receive the Body and Blood of the Lord do so without realizing that the Lord who is received unites the assembly in himself as one body.

Breaking of the Bread

One of the most ancient names by which Christians called the Mass was "the breaking of the bread." This designation is found already in the Acts of the Apostles (Acts 2:46). There was a practical dimension to this action. It was necessary to break the one loaf of bread into various pieces so that it could be shared among those present, but this practical action was immediately seen as a metaphor for the deeper reality that was unfolding. Saint Paul said it in a way that marked the community's consciousness ever since: "Is not the bread we break a sharing in the body of Christ? Because the loaf of bread is one, we, many though we are, are one body, for we all partake of the one loaf" (1 Corinthians 10:16–17). There is a play here between one and the many. Many are made one by sharing the one loaf; that is, the one body of Christ. With the bread being understood to be the body of Christ, it was not possible to break the bread without seeing in this ritual action an image of the Lord's Body on the cross being "broken" in order to give us life, to be distributed to us. This is already implied in the way the evangelists report the Lord's action and words at the Last Supper, summarized in the words as we use them in the institution narrative: " . . . broke the bread and gave it to them, saying . . . / 'This is my Body.'"

So, at one and the same time we have an action in the liturgy that is very practical—arranging for the actual distribution of the consecrated bread and wine to all the faithful—and extremely suggestive on a symbolic level. While all this is going on, the assembly sings a beautiful hymn, the words of which open up further this symbolic dimension. We sing, *Agnus Dei*, "Lamb of God," and are addressing Jesus himself by this title. He is our Passover Lamb whose Body has been sacrificed, whose Blood has been poured out for the forgiveness of our sins. We acknowledge this: "Lamb of God, you take away the sins of the world, . . . " and we ask him for mercy. This is repeated as many times as is necessary to accompany the action of preparation. On the last time we ask for the even larger gift for which we have already prayed: "Grant us peace." This hymn is the same song sung eternally in the feast of heaven which the apostle reported in the book of Revelation: "As my vision continued, I heard the voices of many angels who surrounded the throne and the living creatures and the elders. They were countless in number, thousands and tens of thousands, and they cried out, 'Worthy is the Lamb that was slain!'" (Revelation 5:11–12). Or again, "This is the wedding day of the

Lamb . . . .Happy are they who have been invited to the wedding feast of the Lamb!" (Revelation 19:7, 9).

COMMUNION

Next, the sacred gifts are distributed. To begin this awesome moment the priest holds up before the people the *broken* bread and, as one declaring a huge mystery, tells the people to fix their gaze on it. He says, "Behold the Lamb of God," using the same phrase that the people have been singing. He continues with their same phrase, "behold him who takes away the sins of the world." His actions and his words want to insist. What appears as broken bread you see before you, what appears as wine poured out in your presence—this is nothing less than Christ himself among us come as our food, come among us in the form of the sacrifice that takes our sins away. Then he declares—and how rightly!—"[B]lessed are those called to the supper of the Lamb." This is the supper of the Lamb of which the book of Revelation speaks, the eternal heavenly banquet already begun, the wedding feast of the Lamb! All the people pray together directly to Christ who is held up before them and borrow their words from the centurion who had asked Jesus to cure his paralyzed son: "Lord, I am not worthy that you should come under my roof, but only say the word and my soul shall be healed" (Matthew 8:8). Our Eucharist was foreshadowed in Jesus' healing of the centurion's son!

I said at the beginning of this chapter that we can think of this whole liturgical unit as containing, first, the *words* of the Lord's Prayer and then *actions*, which quite literally enact what has been said and implied in words. Now the community enacts the prayer and forms a procession. While singing with one voice (many are one), all come forward to the priest to receive from him, one by one, the Body and Blood of the Lord. This action confirms in our flesh what our lips have prayed. Once again it is worth our paying close attention to the bread and wine that we originally brought forward. In the same place where it was originally handed over to Christ and from the same hands that received it, it is now handed back to us. (If extraordinary ministers help the priest in this distribution, it is for practical reasons. But the priest always stands at the center and distributes and so is a sacramental sign of Christ himself distributing.) We can say that the lives we brought forward are handed back, but they are handed back completely transfigured and transformed. Into what? The simple ritual words bluntly tell us: "The Body of Christ . . . / The Blood of Christ." We say, "Amen" to express our belief but also to ratify the exchange, to say that we agree to it, that we accept its consequences. We accept becoming ourselves the Body of Christ, ourselves his Blood.

Saint Augustine used to love to preach this dimension of receiving Communion. He said to his congregation, "So, if you want to understand the body of Christ, listen to the apostle telling the faithful, *You, though, are the body of Christ and its members* (1 Corinthians 12:27). If it is you that are the Body of Christ and its members, it is the mystery meaning you that has been placed on the Lord's table; what you receive is the mystery that means you" (Augustine, Sermon 272. PL 38, 1247. English trans. from *The Works of Saint Augustine, Sermons III/7 (230-272B) on the Liturgical Seasons,* trans. and notes, Edmund Hill, OP (New Rochelle: New City Press, 1993), 300). Or: "This sacrament, after all, doesn't present you with the body of Christ in such a way as to divide you from it. This, as the apostle reminds us, was foretold in holy scripture: *they shall be two in one flesh* (Genesis 2:24). This, he says, *is a great sacrament; but I mean in Christ and in the church* (Ephesians 5:32). And in another place he says about this Eucharist itself, *We, though many, are one loaf, one body* (1 Corinthians 10:17). So you are beginning to receive what you have also begun to be, provided you do not receive unworthily" (Augustine, Sermon 228 B. MA *[Miscellanea Agostiniana]* 1, 18–20. English trans. Edmund Hill, Sermons III/6 (184–229Z), 262).

I have called the Communion Rite the revelation of Love, the context in which Love is absolutely defined. We can see this more clearly if we use the word *form* to describe different levels of reality that intersect here. There is the very *form* of God himself intersecting with the liturgical *form* of our receiving Communion. In commenting on the two words *Our Father* in the Lord's Prayer, we saw that eternal love has this very definite *form*: the form of a Father begetting a Son and a Spirit who proceeds from this same love. If this eternal love is to be manifested in the flesh, as it is in the mystery of the Incarnation, then it will be in this same form. That form is the Eucharistic mystery. The words of Jesus himself make this connection between forms: "Just as I have life because of the Father, so the one who feeds on me will have life because of me" (John 6:57). "There is no greater love than this: to lay down one's life for one's friends. You are my friends . . . . I call you friends since I have made known to you all that I heard from my Father" (John 15:13–15). We could perhaps comment by saying that there is no greater love than a God who from all eternity is a Father begetting a Son, and that the form this love takes in manifesting itself to us in the flesh is Jesus' laying down his life for his friends. This same form is expressed in the liturgical act of receiving Communion, receiving the Lord's Body and Blood from his very hands. In all this there is a revelation: "I have made known to you all that I heard from my Father." This is Love. It is Love come among us in the flesh. It is Love being Love by handing over everything. "Though he was in the *form* of God . . . he took the *form* of a slave" (Philippians 2:5–6). This exchange of forms is the form expressed also in this liturgical moment. The one who was crucified for us is God himself; he hands himself over in the form of a slave, in the form of bread and wine.

The Son eternally begotten of the Father and the Spirit who proceeds from this love may both be considered to have their being from a self emptying of the Father. If eternal love manifested in the flesh is to be in this same form (cf. Philippians 2:5–6), it will mean that what we can expect to see in the incarnate Son is a self emptying that begets another like himself, another to whom he has given everything that is his ("I have given them the glory you gave me" John 17:22). The name for this other is Church—and every individual believer in whom, precisely through receiving Communion, the Church mysteriously and mystically subsists. The Holy Spirit is likewise present with his own act of self emptying at the self emptying of the incarnate Word. "The love of God has been poured out in our hearts through the Holy Spirit who has been given to us" (Romans 5:5). The begetting of another in the image of the Son—the Son who is the image of the Father (see Colossians 1:15)—is what is manifested in the reception of Communion.

This other begotten in the image of Christ is, as I have said, the Church. But I do not mean here somehow just vaguely the Church as some freefloating abstraction. I mean very concretely this particular assembly being constituted as Church precisely in this Eucharistic action. In some mysterious way the Eucharist precedes the Church; the Eucharist makes the Church to be. The Eucharist has priority over the Church in the dynamic that constitutes it because only in the Eucharist—the Eucharist which culminates in the Communion Rite that we are now examining—do we have the sign, the effective sign, of that which causes the Church to be what she is; namely, the one begotten by the self emptying of Son and Spirit, "one body, one spirit in Christ."

The notion of oneness is essential to understanding correctly what we are saying here. The reception of Communion is not merely the coincidental juxtaposition of so many individual believers, each of whom is sacramentally united with the Lord in his Body and Blood. It is all those individuals being constituted as one body, and as one body—*only* as one body!—united with the body's head, Christ, and animated by the one Spirit who has raised this body, the Church, from the dead. In this oneness that is accomplished by the reception of

Communion by all and in the sign which is thus made, we can then see in the Church the sign, the image, of the Holy Trinity; that is, many who are one. And within this Trinitarian dynamic we occupy a specific place, the place of the Son. The name for this—we have come full circle from where we started—is love. "Love then consists in this: not that we have loved God, but that he has loved us and has sent his Son as an offering for our sins" (1 John 4:10).

Prayer After Communion

After all the people have received Communion and the Communion chant is complete, there follows a period of silent prayer. This silence is similar to the silence we noted which followed the reading of the Word of God. There, struck with awe at the fact that God should speak to us, our first response was silence. Now our silence is even deeper, for we are struck with awe at the entire mystery of our faith concentrated into what has just happened; namely, that the eternal Son should become incarnate and share himself with us in this most intimate of ways. In this silence, of course, we reflect on what has been accomplished, conversing in our hearts in a profoundly personal way with Christ, "the Son of God who loved me and gave himself up for me" (Galatians 2:20).

There are two beautiful prayers in the large book from which the priest prays, which are printed there just to aid his own devotion at the moment of receiving Communion. And so they are not generally known among the faithful. But those prayers can be a wonderful indicator of how we might speak to Jesus in this moment. "May the receiving of your Body and Blood, / Lord Jesus Christ, / not bring me to judgment and condemnation, / but through your loving mercy / be for me protection in mind and body / and a healing remedy." Or, "free me by this, your most holy Body and Blood, / from all my sins and from every evil; / keep me always faithful to your commandments, / and never let me be parted from you. . . ."

In such silent prayer, especially when it is allowed to sink down deeply into the assembly, there must be a tremendous richness to the prayer that silently moves in each believer's heart. What might we see and hear if we knew the touching ways in which each person was praying in these moments? And yet, even if the prayer is intensely personal and unique to each one, that intensity and uniqueness do not divide the assembly into so many different individuals who have no connection to one another. On the contrary, the communion with each other is increased through the uniqueness of each prayer, for the levels of the apostle's words deepen in wave after wave: "We, though many, are one body." "There are different gifts, but the same Spirit" (1 Corinthians 12:12; 12:4).

This great diversity is pulled into one in the prayer that closes this whole liturgical unit, called rather unimaginatively but with useful precision, the Prayer after Communion. The priest says, "Let us pray," and the assembly as one stands again. Using some phrase or image from the feast or the day in question, the priest prays that the sacrament bear fruit in us and that we remain faithful to all that we have received. The "Amen" of the people is said immediately in response to this prayer, but it is an Amen that closes the entire unit that began with the Lord's Prayer.

Chapter Seven

The Concluding Rites

This will be the shortest chapter of the book. At first glance, setting off as an entire chapter the several pages that comprise it can seem simply to unbalance the orderly profile of the whole, but only in this way can it be made clear that another unit is beginning which is not part of the Communion Rite as such. Short as it is, this chapter is in some sense the biggest for the way in which it opens outward into our actual lives in the world, into life after Mass.

The final unit of the Mass is called the Concluding Rites. It is a very short unit, but an extremely important one. If we understand what is happening in it, its brevity will not prevent us from grasping all that it means. If "Amen" is a signal that a liturgical unit is ending, the repetition of the greeting "The Lord be with you" is a sign that a new one is opening. The priest has said this before. It isn't that he thinks it didn't work the first, the second, or the third time; it is part of the rite, the serious play that lets us know we are starting to do something different now. When the people say again, "And with your spirit," they are reminding the priest to be aware of the priestly grace within him for what he is about to do.

The Mass ends as it began; namely, under the sign of the cross and "in the name of the Father, and of the Son, and of the Holy Spirit." The priest traces in blessing over the assembly a large sign of the cross, saying, "May almighty God bless you, / the Father, and the Son, and the Holy Spirit." As he does so, the people mark again the sign on their bodies and say, "Amen" to the blessing. It is not necessary for me to repeat all that I said at the beginning about the sign of the cross and the Trinitarian name of God, but it is necessary to recall it all here.

The sign of the cross and the holy name of God—Father, Son, and Holy Spirit—are the frame and the seal, the beginning and the end, of the whole Eucharistic rite. The entire rite is about our sharing in our very bodies in the mystery of the Cross, and this sharing reveals to us the mystery of the Trinity. If, at the beginning, this sign and the threefold name of God were our door of entry into the mystery, at the end the sign and the name are a blessing for us. But they are not only a blessing; they are also a task.

After the blessing, the priest or the deacon, in some short phrase, dismisses the people, sending them out. But this dismissal ought not to be understood simply as the banal announcement that "it's over; you can go home now." It needs to be grasped within the dynamic of Jesus' words, "As the Father has sent me, so I send you" (John 20:21; 17:18). This "as" and "so" express a huge mystery; indeed, nothing less than an echo of the Trinitarian mystery in which the Son comes forth from the Father. In that same way, from those same mysterious depths, this assembly comes forth now from the risen Lord and is sent into the world. Thus, the pattern according to which the Lord entered the world must become the pattern for how every Christian comes into the world after celebrating Eucharist. Now the assembly has been made Church, and this is the Church in the world.

In Latin, the words used for centuries for the dismissal have been *Ite missa est,* and from this the whole Eucharistic celebration derives one of its names, "the Mass," from *missa.* It is as if to call the whole celebration by the name of its ultimate purpose, "The Sending." Yet if the Church is sent into the world in the same way that the Son is sent, then that sending implies likewise a self-emptying. Obviously—though we must pause to observe it—the Church has nothing to offer the world if she herself is not first transformed and made into the one body of Christ in whom she partakes of Trinitarian life. "I have told you everything I have heard from my Father," Jesus said to his disciples, and then immediately adds, "It was not you who chose me, but I who chose you and appointed you to go and bear fruit, fruit that will remain" (John 15:15–16). So it is not merely a message, some "word," some "take" on life that the Church offers to the world. In the end it is Christ himself, the eternal Son of the Father, carried now in the flesh and in the lives of his members, poured out in self-emptying love. This is what it means to be a kingdom of priests. Through communion in the Body and Blood of Christ, the whole Church and each member become for the world what Christ is for the world: "life-giving Spirit" (1 Corinthians 15:45). And the Church becomes this in the same pattern whereby Christ and the Spirit are this; namely, a complete self emptying. "No one has greater love than this" (John 15:13) and only love is credible to the world that does not yet believe.

A Summary

At Mass, a great event from the past is proclaimed by means of words and ritual actions. That event is the Death of Jesus of Nazareth and his Resurrection from the dead. In virtue of the Resurrection, the very telling of the event causes what once happened to be present now as the event happening at Mass. This event draws into itself the believers who recount and celebrate it. What happened to Jesus happened to him in his Body. He died in his Body and rose in his Body. The believers who proclaim this event are drawn into his one body, formed into his one body, given communion in his one body. This body is offered as a living sacrifice of praise and thanksgiving to the God and Father who raised Jesus from the dead. Every moment of the Mass, every word and every movement, big and small, combine together to accomplish this proclamation that becomes sacrificial offering.

Lightning Source UK Ltd.
Milton Keynes UK
UKHW011905310121
378006UK00004B/19